The Prince with the play-boy's reputation pursued the beautiful actress who epitomized Hollywood stardom: Aly Khan and Rita Hayworth's love affair was deeply passionate and tempestuous. But all she wanted was a happy home life. Instead, jealous scenes and extravagant reconciliations finally wrecked their dreams.

DARK DESTINIES

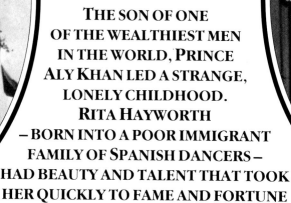

Hulton Picture Company

Kobal Collection

**THE SON OF ONE
OF THE WEALTHIEST MEN
IN THE WORLD, PRINCE
ALY KHAN LED A STRANGE,
LONELY CHILDHOOD.
RITA HAYWORTH
– BORN INTO A POOR IMMIGRANT
FAMILY OF SPANISH DANCERS –
HAD BEAUTY AND TALENT THAT TOOK
HER QUICKLY TO FAME AND FORTUNE**

♛ *Although born into vastly different circumstances, both Aly and Rita were the children of mothers with theatrical backgrounds. Teresa, with Aly above, was a professional ballet dancer when she first met the Aga Khan in 1908. She came from a comparatively humble home and was understandably flattered when her striking beauty caught the attention of so rich and famous a public figure. Rita's mother had performed in the Ziegfeld Follies and in musical comedy, and came to resent the interruption to her stage career that followed the arrival of children. Her father, Eduardo, however, derived much pleasure from little Margarita, photographed above right with him in 1919*

THE EXTRAORDINARY PATTERN OF FATE which was to lead Rita Hayworth to world stardom, and a passionate but disastrous marriage to Prince Aly Salomone Khan, began on 11 October 1918. She was born in Brooklyn, New York, and christened Margarita Carmen Cansino, eldest child of Eduardo Cansino and Volga Haworth.

The Dancing Cansinos

Eduardo was a handsome dancer who had emigrated from Spain to the United States with his sister, Elisa, in 1913. They were born survivors. Arriving with just $20 between them and speaking little English, they earned a living by performing traditional Spanish dances. By 1915 they had caught the public imagination with their sensuous, exciting act, were topping vaudeville bills around the country and earning a salary of $1500 a week.

Broadway beckoned, and in 1916 the Dancing Cansinos were appearing in a top New York musical, *Follow Me*. Here Eduardo met Volga Haworth, a 19-year-old Irish-American

showgirl. Strong-willed, extrovert and ambitious, Volga had rebelled against her family by running away to go on stage when she was 16 years old. In 1917, she caused them further grief by marrying Eduardo much against her family's wishes.

For a few years, everything seemed to go well and Eduardo's career scaled new heights. Volga then gave birth to two sons – Eduardo, a year after Margarita in 1919, and Vernon in 1922. But her frustrated theatrical ambitions began to gnaw away at her, and she started drinking. Sadly, this habit eventually led to what her children innocently called her 'illness' and within ten years she had become a borderline alcoholic.

Margarita was a quiet little girl who adored her father and longed to please him. Despite her endearing plumpness, she soon revealed the family talent for dancing and was enrolled in her uncle's New York dancing school. Not that she had any say in the matter; her father wanted her to learn, and so she was sent to classes. She was just four years old.

East meets West

By curious coincidence, Prince Aly Khan was also born with the theatre in his blood. His maternal grandmother, Rosa, came from an Italian family of vaudeville entertainers. Teresa Magliano, his beautiful mother, was a 19-year-old ballet dancer when, in 1908, she met the 31-year-old Aga Khan III in Monte Carlo. This graceful, delicate-looking girl enchanted the Aga from the first moment he set eyes on her.

The Aga Khan was already a married man. In 1897 he had married a cousin, Shahzadi, in India amid extraordinary celebrations which lasted 16 days. However, their union was an uneasy one, arranged by his mother, and it soon began to show signs of strain. As he later explained, 'We were both ignorant and innocent . . . inevitably we drifted apart.'

Travelling around Europe, the Aga Khan discovered freedom and cultivated a taste for Western women. For many sophisticated ladies, he was a fascinating proposition: fabulously wealthy, with exquisite taste and great style, he was also the spiritual leader for millions of his Ismaili Muslim followers. Teresa, whose father restored furniture and church frescoes, was easily swept off her feet. The Aga installed her in a luxurious suite at Monte Carlo's famous Hotel de Paris and her dancing career was soon brought to an end, for within a year she gave birth to their first son, Mahdi.

'I had wanted a boy . . . What could I do with a girl?'

EDUARDO ON RITA

Twenty-two-year-old Teresa was already pregnant again when little Mahdi died of meningitis, aged 18 months. Distraught and unwell, she returned home to Turin. There she gave birth to her second child on 17 June 1911. It was a difficult birth for mother and baby. The birth certificate read in part, ' . . . from the union of Teresa Magliano, unmarried . . . with His Highness The Aga Khan, son of the late Aga Ali Shah, 34 years old, born at Karachi, living at Monte Carlo, was born a male baby . . . to whom are given the names of Aly Salomone.'

Baby Aly was the centre of his young mother's world. Teresa was often lonely, despite being surrounded by her Italian family, for the Aga Khan spent very little time with her. His material generosity to Teresa — four houses in her own name, and a large allowance — was in sharp contrast to the scant attention he

usually paid to her.

Teresa and Aly travelled annually among the houses Aly would one day inherit: rue de Prony in Paris, Villa Terpsichore in Nice, a country house at Maisons-Lafitte and the Villa Gorizia on the sea front at Deauville.

Educating Rita

Until he was 13, Aly received a sketchy education from a succession of governesses. Little Margarita's schooling was even more inadequate. Her illiterate father had never attended a school and did not see why his daughter should. However, her mother stood firm and for a few short years Rita went to school — first

♛ *The Dancing Cansinos, Eduardo and his sister Elisa below, were much in demand soon after they arrived in the USA in 1913. Their performances of Spanish dance were colourful and exciting, earning them big money. But the coming of the talkies in the late 1920s adversely affected their careers*

in New York, and later in California. One report of the time described her as 'kind and sweet, sometimes below average ability'.

The Cansinos had made the gruelling trip west in an old truck in 1927. That year represented a crucial turning point in the movie industry: the arrival of sound. Eduardo, dreaming of stardom, decided that his future lay in Hollywood, ignoring the fact that his fractured

♛ **Below** *Rita aged five, Vernon (far left) aged two, and Eduardo, Jnr (known as Sonny) aged four. On Rita's birth her father had said he had wanted a boy, but it was Rita rather than her brothers who showed most promise of following in his dancing footsteps, and he focused his ever-demanding eye on her*

atlantic city · N.J.
aug 1924 –

Kobal Collection

AP/Wide World Photos

English was a major disadvantage. By 1929, with spectacularly bad timing, he had opened a dancing school, which inevitably suffered as a result of the Wall Street crash in the same year. His most constant pupil turned out to be his plump, withdrawn daughter whom he taught regularly after school.

Dancing partners

By the time she was 12, Rita was partnering her 36-year-old father and the Dancing Cansinos had been resurrected to earn some badly

♛ *At the age of ten Rita right was already a seasoned dancer, having been sent by her father to classes from the age of four. By 1929 Eduardo had relocated the family from New York to Los Angeles and had opened a dancing school on Sunset Boulevard. He remained ambitious for his daughter, and when circumstances compelled him to take to the boards again he did so with Rita as his partner*

needed money for the family. This was the Prohibition era, and Rita and her father entertained the pleasure-seeking Americans who flocked to the floating casinos off the California coast. These establishments managed to evade the strict anti-alcohol and gambling laws by staying outside the three-mile limit. Yet although they were earning a living, Eduardo frequently made Rita catch fish for their supper, rather than pay for any food for himself and his daughter. She was so in awe of his uncertain temper that she obeyed unquestioningly. Eduardo and Rita also worked in a popular nightclub in Tijuana, just across the California border in Mexico, a crossing she remembered making on her 13th birthday.

Childhood traumas

Rita's hair was dyed black and drawn back into a Spanish-style bun and she wore Spanish clothes. She was kept locked in her dressing room between appearances, while her father drank and gambled away much of what they had earned. He was often violent when drunk, and Rita became increasingly afraid of him.

It was a strange and lonely life for a young girl. She was no longer allowed to go to school or to mix with other children. When she was not working she spent hours rehearsing with her autocratic father. His fierce possessiveness was unnatural and unhealthy. In later years Rita would claim that she had been sexually abused by him in her early teens. A childhood friend of her brothers recalled how Eduardo would scream at his daughter, 'Don't do that! Don't be so stupid!' Her brief childhood stolen, Rita grew ever more silent. Her only outlet for self-expression was dancing.

A visit to India

Aly's early adolescence was also a time of upheaval and change. His father was growing old and, since he was still officially married to the Begum Shahzadi, he had no heir. Shahzadi lived in Bombay, where she hid from the world behind the veils of purdah. She had not seen her husband since 1907. However, Muslim law allows for four wives and, in the absence of a son to succeed him, the 46-year-old Aga Khan would seem to have had little choice but to marry Teresa.

And so, on 23 January 1923, Teresa and the Aga Khan were married quietly in Bombay. Eleven-year-old Aly was enchanted and astounded by his trip to India. He visited his grandmother, Lady Ali Shah, whose imposing home was situated in the Malabar Hills. Grandmother herself proved to be equally imposing, for she succeeded in running her son's empire with considerable aplomb during his prolonged absences in Europe.

AUGUST IN DEAUVILLE

In the early part of the 20th century – both before and after World War 1 – it was extremely fashionable to pass the sultry days of August on the Normandy coast, and above all at Deauville. Here aristocrats and upper-class Parisians mingled with the bohemian set, and many a summer romance blossomed on the broad white sands.

The Aga Khan lived with his unofficial family for only three weeks a year. These often awkward days were spent at the Villa Gorizia which he had given to Teresa Magliano and which was subsequently inherited by Aly Khan.

Colourful theatrical stars of the day such as Maurice Chevalier, the seductive, leggy Mistinguett and the flirtatious Dolly Sisters were regular visitors. They all knew the Aga.

It was here that Aly learned to ride, played tennis and was alternately showered with gifts or scolded by his forbidding father

Jean-Loup Charmet

The Ismaili population of Bombay were delighted by their leader's visit. Thousands came to pay homage, give offerings of gold, and seek the blessing of the Imam. For the first time, Aly saw his father assume the role of spiritual leader and King. It was like something out of a storybook. Shedding his customary western clothes, the Aga took a ceremonial perfumed bath, donned an embroidered robe, golden slippers and astrakhan hat, and graciously received his followers in the gardens of Aga Hall. This promised to be Aly's inheritance.

🜲 *In 1930, four years after Aly's mother had died, his father, the Aga Khan III, leader of the Ismaili Muslims, married his third wife, Andrée. Their son, Sadruddin, was born in 1933 below. Later Andrée was to recall how Aly was 'always so charming. Who knows if he was happy or not? He was all mixed up, but I never knew what was bothering him'*

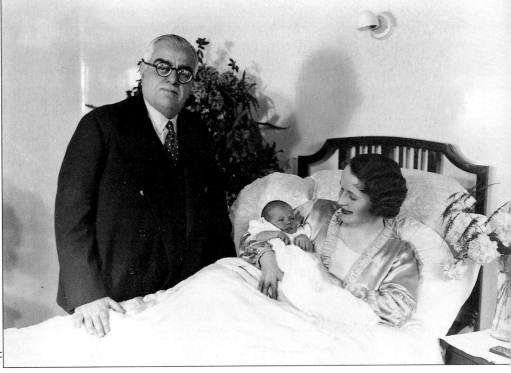

Popperfoto

ALY GROWS UP

Realizing that he had neglected his son's education, the Aga Khan decided that Aly should go to England for this purpose. He turned to Oxford-educated Charles Waddington, a classics scholar, horseman, retired Colonel and principal of a college for the sons of Indian Royalty. After long service in India he had retired to live in England. Waddington was now appointed Aly's guardian, and entrusted with his education until such time as he was ready to go to Cambridge. At least, that was the plan. But Aly's undoubted intelligence was marred by lack of concentration and he never fulfilled his father's hopes of academic glory.

His talents were of a different type. Aly was a fearless rider, handling horses with tremendous flair. He hunted regularly in Sussex and Warwickshire, where his daring exploits in the field won him many friends. He learned how to judge a horse's qualities, and loved to ride his father's thoroughbreds as an amateur, but extremely promising, jockey.

This English idyll was cruelly disrupted by the sudden death of his mother in 1926. Devastated and shaken, Aly attended her funeral at the Paris mosque. He returned, heartbroken, to the Waddington family home and barely spoke of his mother to anyone again.

Three years later, another shock awaited

THE LEADER OF HIS PEOPLE

The Ismailis are a Muslim sect, headed by the Aga Khan – also known as the Imam – who is descended from the Prophet Muhammad's son-in-law.

The Aga Khans are all-powerful, responsible for both the spiritual and temporal well-being of their followers. The centuries-old custom of paying tribute to the Imam with gifts of gold, money and property has resulted in the accumulation of enormous wealth, which has been returned to the followers – by both the present Aga and his grandfather – in the form of trust funds, banks offering favourable interest rates, schools and economic investment.

When he was enthroned in a ceremony in Dar-es-Salaam in October 1957, the present Imam (Karim Aga Khan) *left* was given the large engraved signet ring that served as a seal of authority during the 12th and 13th centuries, and a historic chain of 49 links

♛ *Times were difficult for Eduardo in the early years of the Depression. Few people could afford dancing lessons, and work in Hollywood was hard to find. So he revived the Dancing Cansinos: this time, Rita took the place of his sister. Kept busy in casinos and clubs in both California and Mexico, Eduardo and his teenage daughter* below *cut quite a dash*

the young Prince. His father, by now divorced from Shahzadi, remarried. This time his bride was a Frenchwoman, Andrée, whom he had known for more than ten years. Aly took the news badly and it would be many years before he accepted his stepmother.

Aly now began what was to be a life-long pattern – he threw himself headlong into the pursuit of pleasure. He bought a little place in London's Mayfair, gave and attended wild parties, and was a regular visitor at the chic Embassy Club in Bond Street. He fell madly in love with a striking débutante, Margaret Whigham – the future Duchess of Argyll. Romantically, he was determined to marry her. However, her father's racial prejudice caused him to reject the dark-skinned boy. Margaret, 'utterly miserable', was forbidden to see her unofficial fiancé. Six months later, Aly left for his first tour of the East as the Aga Khan's heir apparent, and Margaret was left behind.

A string of affairs

Aly's love of women seemed impossible to satisfy. Even when he was in love with one particular woman, he was incapable of remaining faithful. As his reputation as an exciting lover grew, so did his list of conquests. Not typically handsome, he was 5ft 8in tall, had receding dark hair (he began losing hair in his early twenties), an olive complexion and warm dark brown eyes.

So what was it? It seems he had enormous charm, and an uncanny instinct for what a woman wanted. 'When he fell in love with a woman, it was madly and deeply. The only

UPI/Bettmann Newsphotos

Camera Press

Popperfoto

♔ **Aly** left *inherited the refined good looks of his mother combined with the Oriental allure of his father. In his teens, he went to live in England with an English family who oversaw his education by private tutors. He had early displayed a dreamy, distracted temperament but was also capable of intense activity. Thomas Waddington, son of Aly's English guardian, remembered the Prince as easily bored. 'He was restless, both physically and mentally,' he said. Later, Aly established himself as an eligible man about town in London, where one of his most intense liaisons was with the equally exciting Margaret Whigham* above, *later Duchess of Argyll; he was not yet 20. Born in Scotland but raised in the USA, Margaret was the best-known débutante to be presented at Court in 1930 and a dazzling adornment to the social scene. She was smitten with Aly, but their relationship foundered on her father's disapproval*

♛ *Aly married Mrs Joan Guinness, soon after her divorce, in a quiet civil ceremony in Paris in 1936.* **Below** *The bridal party outside the town hall:* **from left** *the Aga, Aly, Sadruddin, Joan, her mother and the Begum*

thing, it might last only one night,' said Hollywood gossip columnist and socialite, Elsa Maxwell. An affair with Aly soon became the fashionable thing among the fast-living set, for as one woman was later to admit, 'It was considered the chic thing to do. You weren't in the swim . . . if you'd not been to bed with Aly.'

His ardent courtship of Lady Thelma Furness, then mistress of the Prince of Wales, gave rise to plenty of gossip. Aly met the beautiful American in New York, just before she was due to return to England and the Prince. He pursued her, filled her cabin with roses, but initially only succeeded in amusing her.

Once reunited with her Prince, however, Lady Furness discovered that her close friend Wallis Simpson had superseded her in his affections. He pretended to be jealous of Aly's extravagant attentions to her, making it clear that Thelma was no longer the Royal favourite. It was a cruel blow.

Betrayed by one of her best friends and rejected by her beloved 'little man', Thelma joined Aly in Paris. They spent the whole summer of 1934 enjoying themselves in Spain, Ireland and at Deauville. It was at Deauville that Aly met Mrs Joan Guinness, who was holidaying alone – her husband, Loel, being too busy to join her. In less than two years Mrs Guinness was to divorce her husband, amid much scandal, and become Aly's first wife. Something he later said about their association reveals just how confused the young man was: 'I had been involved with several women. I was tired of trouble. Joan was a sane and solid sort of girl and I thought if I married her, I would stay out of trouble.'

Hulton Picture Company

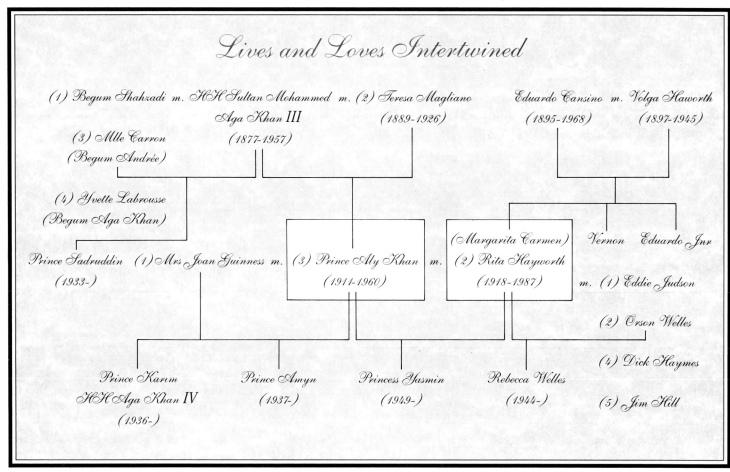

Lives and Loves Intertwined

(1) Begum Shahzadi m. H H Sultan Mohammed m. (2) Teresa Magliano   Eduardo Cansino m. Volga Haworth
Aga Khan III   (1889-1926)   (1895-1968)   (1897-1945)

(3) Mlle Carron   (1877-1957)
(Begum Andrée)

(4) Yvette Labrousse
(Begum Aga Khan)

Prince Sadruddin   (1) Mrs Joan Guinness m.   (3) Prince Aly Khan   m.   (Margarita Carmen)   Vernon   Eduardo Jnr
(1933-)   (1914-1960)   (2) Rita Hayworth   m. (1) Eddie Judson
(1918-1987)

(2) Orson Welles

(4) Dick Haymes

Prince Karim   Prince Amyn   Princess Yasmin   Rebecca Welles
H H Aga Khan IV   (1937-)   (1949-)   (1944-)   (5) Jim Hill
(1936-)

First steps to stardom

While Aly was busy charming high-society ladies, 15-year-old Rita was facing her first Hollywood screen test. It was not a success, but she was nevertheless given some small parts as an extra. Then she was spotted by Winfield Sheehan, production chief at Fox Studios. A second screen test revealed Rita's ability to project her sexuality on film and she was given a part dancing in a Spencer Tracy movie, *Dante's Inferno*, released in 1935. Three more films followed in the same year – and each time Rita played an exotic, foreign character.

U PI/Bettmann Newsphotos

UPI/Bettmann Newsphotos

Around this time, Rita attracted the dubious attention of a much older man named Eddie Judson. This 39-year-old wheeler-dealer had been married three times before coming to Hollywood. Nobody really knew how he earned a living, but he always seemed to have plenty of money.

When, due to a takeover, Fox Studios became Twentieth Century-Fox, Rita's contract was not renewed. Eddie Judson wasted no time in exploiting this opportunity. He convinced Rita's family that he could find her a new employer, and gradually began to take over their daughter's life. He told her what to wear, and encouraged her to change her name to something that sounded more American. She added a 'y' to her mother's maiden name, Haworth, and Rita Hayworth was born.

In early 1937, Columbia Pictures offered Rita a seven-year 'starlet's contract'. By now, the 18-year-old was completely under Judson's shady spell. That May, they eloped to Arizona where they were married. Rita, with hindsight, was to say, 'I married him for love, but he married me for an investment.' Certainly, it was an investment he regarded very seriously. He took charge, and began to alter the way Rita walked, talked, dressed and behaved. She became – to a large extent – his creation.

Eddie worked hard to make sure Rita was noticed by those who mattered in the film industry. He hired expensive dresses for her to wear, and took her out to all the fashionable nightspots. Rita's hard-earned money paid for all this, of course. He badgered her to lose weight, and had her natural hairline altered and 'improved' by painful electrolysis. Her own dark brown hair was lightened to a warm auburn shade.

The concentrated effort paid off. In 1939, Rita appeared in her first important movie, *Only Angels Have Wings*, starring Cary Grant and directed by the legendary Howard Hawks. She was on her way at last.

👑 *Although she had earlier managed to secure a few bit parts, Rita's film career only really took off after she met Eddie Judson, a sharply dressed, fast-talking charmer who set about exploiting her potential. He dominated his new charge, changing her appearance and moulding her into the popular image of a potential star. And it worked. Rita was offered a 'starlet's contract' by Columbia in 1937 and was soon being promoted by the studio's publicity machine* left. *Rita and Judson married that year* above. *She was 18, he was 41*

'I married him for love, but he married me for an investment'

RITA ON EDDIE JUDSON

An exciting motion picture experience you'll remember for years!

RITA HAYWORTH
GENE KELLY

Cover Girl
in *Technicolor*

with

LEE BOWMAN · PHIL SILVERS · JINX FALKENBURG
and

THE COVER GIRLS 15 of America's Most Beautiful Women

Screen Play by VIRGINIA VAN UPP
Directed by CHARLES VIDOR

A
COLUMBIA PICTURE

Music by
JEROME KERN
Lyrics by
IRA GERSHWIN

♛ The film version of *Salome* (right), a Technicolor extravaganza starring Rita Hayworth and Stewart Granger, was released in 1953. Although the role and the film did not interest Rita, *Salome* was a big box-office success and once again confirmed her enormous appeal to audiences across the country

♛ Rita starred in *Cover Girl* (above) with Gene Kelly, one of Hollywood's star personalities well known for his 'good-guy' characterizations. *Cover Girl*, released in 1944, was just one of the many successful films Rita made for Colombia

♛ *You Were Never Lovelier* (below) was the second film that paired Rita with Fred Astaire. Astaire was a perfectionist and worked Rita incredibly hard. But she was rewarded with his praises: 'She's really remarkable,' he said

Columbia Pictures presents
RITA   ORSON
HAYWORTH · WELLES
The LADY *from*
SHANGHAI
Everett SLOANE and Gloom ANDERS   Directed and Produced by Orson WELLES

♛ *The Lady from Shanghai* (above) was very much Orson Welles's film. Not only did he make Rita cut and dye her hair (to the horror of Columbia), he also filled the film with autobiographical allusions to the guilt he felt over her. In his brilliant hall-of-mirrors scene Rita faces multiple reflections of herself and the father-husband figure who is trying to destroy her

Fred Astaire and Rita Hayworth—dancing and singing together!

FRED   RITA
ASTAIRE ★ HAYWORTH
in
"YOU WERE
NEVER LOVELIER"
A COLUMBIA PICTURE

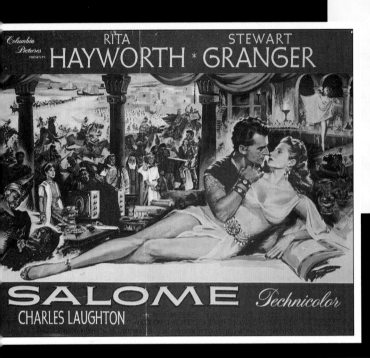

THE LOVE GODDESS

From her early years as an entertainer, it was evident that the sultry Latin beauty, Rita Hayworth, would be moulded into a star. Despite her natural shyness, she proved a fine performer, with the ability to transform herself magically for the camera, and soon became one of Hollywood's leading ladies. Her fiery roles in films like Blood and Sand *and the infamous* Gilda *forever identified her as the sex symbol and 'love goddess' that she never wanted to be*

♛ *Gilda* (below) was to become Rita's signature role. In this *film noir* of 1946, Rita plays the wife of the proprietor of a gambling casino – a sexual temptress who will do anything to arouse the jealousy of her former lover. The best-known scene is Gilda's provocative song and dance number, *Put the Blame on Mame*, in which she does a mock strip tease for a delighted casino audience

Columbia Pictures PRESENTS

RITA HAYWORTH · STEWART GRANGER

SALOME Technicolor

CHARLES LAUGHTON

There NEVER was a woman like...

Gilda

RITA HAYWORTH · GLENN FORD

GEORGE MACREADY · JOSEPH CALLEIA

a Columbia Picture

SCREENPLAY BY MARION PARSONNET
PRODUCED BY VIRGINIA VAN UPP · DIRECTED BY CHARLES VIDOR

LIFE IN THE FAST LANE

THE RICH, FAMOUS AND BEAUTIFUL PEOPLE OF THE INTERNATIONAL SMART SET WERE CONSTANTLY CROSSING PATHS ROUND THE WORLD, AND IT WAS INEVITABLE THAT, SOONER OR LATER, RITA AND ALY WOULD MEET

EIGHT MONTHS AFTER HIS WEDDING TO Joan, Aly became a father for the first time. His son, Karim, was born on 13 December 1936 in Geneva. Exactly nine months later, on 13 September 1937, a second son, Amyn, was born. Joan was determined to be a good wife to Aly. She became a Muslim, studied Persian and Arabic, and shared Aly's love of horses. The family moved around from one glamorous location to another — Bombay, Gstaad, Cairo, Nairobi — and although Aly was unable to resist a few affairs, Joan chose to regard them as meaningless. She fully intended to make her second marriage work.

When war was declared in 1939, Aly impulsively joined the French Foreign Legion and was posted to Beirut. Soon he was working for British Intelligence in Cairo, where he was joined by Joan and his sons. In many ways, life changed very little for the couple. They hosted elaborate dinners and there were dances in the garden. Aly enjoyed meeting a cosmopolitan blend of refugees, old friends and intriguing eccentrics who had all ended up in Cairo.

A dangerous career

Aly's wartime career exposed him to much potential danger. Despite this, he was later to remark, 'You shouldn't say you were happiest while there was a war going on, but I think that's a sentiment a lot of men feel. Those were some of the happiest years of my life.'

During these nomadic years, Aly's marriage to Joan began to fall apart. There were rows and frosty silences. When Joan and the boys left Cairo for Nairobi and safety, their union was effectively at an end. After the war, Joan settled in England while Karim and Amyn were sent to 'the school of kings', Le Rosey in Switzerland. Uncertain about the future, Aly concentrated on horses, becoming his father's

Syndication International

Roger-Viollet

December 1941, when the Japanese bombed Pearl Harbor. Until that time, the war in Europe seemed far away to the average American citizen; it was very much business as usual in the United States.

Rita Hayworth's 1941 had been a glittering success. She had released four films – *The Strawberry Blonde*, *Affectionately Yours*, *Blood and Sand* and *You'll Never Get Rich*. For *You'll Never Get Rich*, Rita worked extremely hard; she was partnering Fred Astaire – perfectionist star and legendary dancer. She was understandably nervous, but Astaire (a hard

'Don't disturb me.

I want to see this

wonderful girl'

ALY WATCHING RITA
IN *BLOOD AND SAND*

taskmaster) was full of praise for his new partner. 'She learned steps faster than anyone I've ever known,' he said approvingly, and called her 'a born dancer'.

Rita's fans responded wildly to the melodramatic *Blood and Sand*. This tempestuous story starred Rita as a predatory *femme fatale* who seduces a handsome bullfighter, and gave her an opportunity to display some sensuous Latin dancing.

♔ *From his early years as a young man in England, Aly left was known as a playboy and a notorious womanizer and, despite his good intentions throughout both his marriages and his many affairs, he continued to live up to this reputation for the rest of his life*

♔ *Rita was, by 1941, already widely known for her dark, sensual screen persona above and was considered a fully fledged leading lady. However, her subsequent roles in the forties, especially her performance in* Gilda, *would launch her into the realm of the major Hollywood stars*

♔ *Within a few years of their marriage, Joan and Aly had had two sons, Prince Karim and Prince Amyn. But the couple drifted apart as his role in World War 2 began to demand more of Aly's attention. By 1941, when Joan and the boys were living in Nairobi right to ensure their safety during the war, Aly had already spotted his future wife in* Blood and Sand

official business partner with responsibility for stables, bloodstock and stud farms.

When the war ended, Aly was a Lieutenant-Colonel in the British Army, stationed in Heidelberg. He knew that the Nazis had stolen some thoroughbred horses from his father's stables in Normandy and set about reclaiming them one by one. He often drove through the night from Germany to France, pulling a horse-box containing one or two valuable animals behind his army jeep.

Most of his energy and enthusiasm now went into building up the family horse business. Tirelessly, he commuted between France, Ireland, the United States and South America. Within three years, he and his father owned four stud farms in France and seven in Ireland. Their horses were estimated to be worth altogether some $8 million.

'A couple of horse traders'

Aly adored buying and selling, and he was still a daring amateur jockey, too. As always, he loved nothing better than a challenge – and this one was to make money in a notoriously risky business. 'After all,' he was to say, 'Father and I are just a couple of horse traders. Some people are in this business for fun; we're in it for profit.'

The USA did not enter World War 2 until

Topham

AP/Wide World Photos

☙ *Rita and Orson's wedding in 1943 came as a surprise to everyone. Rita told no one of her plans, not even her parents, until she announced to the crew of* Cover Girl *that because she was to be married that day, she might be a little late back from lunch. The civil ceremony* above *took place at the Bay City Building in Santa Monica. After they had exchanged their vows before the judge, Orson kissed his bride and together they dashed off to the waiting car which would take Rita back to the studio*

☙ *The marriage was already showing signs of strain when their daughter, Rebecca, was born in 1944* right*. In fact, Rita's fits of rage and jealousy and Orson's obsessional devotion to his work would bring about their separation only a few years after this happy event. But, despite the turbulence of their brief time together, Rita would later refer to Orson as 'the great love of my life'*

Aly Khan saw *Blood and Sand* in wartime Egypt and was captivated by this first glimpse of his future wife. 'Don't disturb me,' he cautioned his friends, who were paying scant attention to the plot. 'I want to see this wonderful girl.' Aly saw *Blood and Sand* three times; he was more than a little in love with Rita's exotic screen persona.

Exploiting a star

The film industry was one of the busiest, and most glamorous, businesses of the decade, and Rita Hayworth was being hailed as an exciting new star. Her beautiful face was everywhere. Publicity stories regularly appeared in dozens of magazines and newspapers. Her husband, Eddie Judson, and her hard-working press agent never stopped pushing her forward. For Judson, Rita had become the biggest business opportunity of his life. Their home was open to the press seven days a week, at his instigation. Rita was afraid of him, and seemed unable to complain. Meekly, she told reporters, 'I owe everything to Ed. I could never have made the grade in Hollywood without him.'

But Judson pushed her loyalty to the limit when he began to suggest that she sleep with other men in order to further her career. 'It

seemed to me that Eddie would have sold his wife to the highest bidder if it would have enhanced her career,' said one close associate at the time. He badgered her to start an affair with Harry Cohn, a powerful executive at Columbia Studios. When Cohn invited the couple for a weekend on his yacht, Judson pretended he was unwell and insisted Rita go alone. This was really the final straw for Rita. She went for the weekend, but made up her mind that she would never give in to Cohn's sexual obsession with her – whatever the cost to her career. He renewed her contract anyway; after all, she was now a big box-office success.

Married to a monster

Meanwhile, Judson was cleverly embezzling much of his wife's large salary. Rita had little grasp of financial matters and allowed Judson to make all their investments. She was also terrified of him, for he regularly threatened to mutilate and disfigure her face.

Rita was working flat out, this time on a film called *My Gal Sal* with a handsome young actor named Victor Mature. His dark good looks, combined with a corny sense of humour and talent for romantic gestures, appealed to Rita. He made her laugh, and never told her what to do. They fell for each other, and the resulting light-hearted affair seemed finally to give her the confidence to break away from the monster she had married.

When Rita instigated divorce proceedings in 1942, her husband responded by taking $25,000 in cash out of their safety-deposit boxes. A messy divorce followed, with Eddie threatening to cite Rita's adultery. Rita's story was splashed all over the papers, despite her

AP/Wide World Photos

pleas for secrecy. Finally, under threat of financial investigation, Eddie backed down and the divorce went through.

On 7 September 1943, Rita married the fascinating, complex and often brilliant Orson Welles. The couple had been involved for about a year before their wedding, and were passionately in love.

Beauty and the Brain

In the beginning, their love affair and marriage seemed like a dream come true. Orson adored Rita, and never talked down to her or patronized her lack of education. She felt loved for herself, not the famous star she had become, for Orson remained unaffected by her image. 'Her essential quality was sweetness,' he once said, and this is what drew him to her.

They worked together for 'The Mercury Wonder Show', an entertainment Orson had created for US troops. Soon, Rita was pregnant, and gave birth to a daughter, Rebecca, on 17 December 1944. But already there were problems. Welles was very ambitious, and spent a great deal of time away from home concentrat-

'When you're in love, you're living, you matter'

RITA

ing on his work. He was also finding her insecurity and irrational fits of jealousy very hard to cope with. She would frequently greet him in tears, convinced that he was seeing other women. Eventually, her fears came true, for he began a number of affairs, notably with singer Judy Garland. Yet to his dying day, he always maintained that he loved her, and blamed his obsession with work for their rift. Rita, in turn, referred to him as 'the love of my life'.

The golden pair Hollywood had nicknamed 'Beauty and the Brain' parted, but were reconciled once more when Orson began making preparations for a new film. *Lady From Shanghai* was a dark, tortuous thriller and starred his wife in the title role. But once they stopped working together the marriage began to disintegrate for the second, and last, time.

Rita was not lonely for long. She began an affair with the recently widowed David Niven, which was inevitably inflated by a gossip-hungry press. Orson Welles consoled himself with Marilyn Monroe. The divorce was brought before the courts in November 1947.

Bettmann/Hulton

ORSON WELLES

Orson Welles had a reputation for daring and originality. He had rocked America with his horrifically realistic radio production of *The War of the Worlds*: countless listeners had panicked, momentarily convinced that Martians had really invaded the Earth. The first two films that Welles directed – *Citizen Kane* and *The Magnificent Ambersons* – have become acknowledged classics.

Citizen Kane (above) caused considerable controversy when it was released, because the story closely followed the career of newspaper magnate William Randolph Hearst. Hearst vented his anger against Welles through his many newspapers, and Hollywood – insecure at the best of times – accused Welles of making trouble for the film industry. Already mistrusted by an industry which now turned against him, his position as youthful genius was badly undermined.

Although this was a blow to his career, Welles's intelligence and drive did not desert him. It was during these uncertain times that he fell in love with Rita, restoring his – and her – self-confidence.

Although the promise of his early career was never really fulfilled, in 1970 he was awarded an Oscar 'for supreme artistry and versatility in the creation of motion pictures'

AP/Wide World Photos

♛ *Following her divorce from Orson, Rita began a secret and serious affair with the millionaire producer-director and playboy Howard Hughes* left. *It wasn't long before she discovered, to her shock, that she was pregnant. Her condition, which would soon cause problems during the filming of* The Loves of Carmen, *was unacceptable to Rita at this point in her life. Despite any inheritance or privileges her child might have acquired from Hughes, Rita could not bear to have a baby out of wedlock and sought a discreet abortion*

Rita, by 1948, was a very famous star. Christened 'the Love Goddess' by *Life* magazine, she continued to make one film after another – although her increasingly mythic status secretly worried her. Of one of her most enduring roles, that of the temptress *Gilda* (1946), she was to say, 'Men go to bed with Gilda, but wake up with me.' For, however confident, sexy, and alluring she appeared on screen, she rarely displayed these qualities in her private life.

A trip to Europe

While playing the role of smouldering gypsy Carmen in *The Loves of Carmen*, Rita began an affair with millionaire tycoon Howard Hughes. The association was eventually to lead her to Europe and Aly Khan. Hughes was a wealthy playboy, pilot and producer-director – later to become a legendary recluse. Their relationship was a serious one, but Rita eventually realized that there was no future in it. Unfortunately, by this time she was pregnant. Since there was no question of having the baby, Rita sought an abortion. A four-month holiday in Europe was planned so that she could recuperate, from both the operation and the punishing work schedule she had been following.

Her companion on this trip, Shifra Haran, had previously worked as secretary for Orson Welles – and was very fond of Rita. In May 1948 the two women set sail for France on a luxury ocean liner. Rita's longing for privacy and hatred of crowds meant that she spent most of the voyage in her cabin. 'We would go walking when it was darkest and when there weren't too many people around,' recalled Shifra.

Once in Paris, complications from the

♛ Second only to women was Aly's love of horses. He adored the risky business of buying and selling horses and was still a proficient amateur jockey when he participated in the 1949 race at St Cloud above. However, his riding skills did not prove good enough that day to pull him out of his position in last place

'Men go to bed with Gilda, but wake up with me'

RITA

♛ The glamorous 'love goddess' of the screen right was the Rita that Aly had first encountered and, at the start, he had 'fallen in love with her beauty and fame'. She was the Hollywood prize he had won. But while he would soon discover her insecurities and feel the need to take care of her, he would never understand her desire to abandon her career

abortion set in. Rita became very ill and was secretly admitted to the American Hospital. The exact reason for her stay was kept quiet. When reporters finally tracked her down they referred in their news stories to anaemia, jaundice and unidentified infections.

Convalescing at the Hotel Lancaster, Rita agreed to appear at a charity ball in the Eiffel Tower. Exquisitely dressed in a brocade gown – specially designed for her by Balmain – and wearing a small fortune in borrowed jewels, Rita gave a short speech in French to her society audience. Everyone agreed she looked stunning. As he watched her from the crowd, Prince Aly Khan thought so too. He very much wanted to meet her as soon as possible. And what Aly Khan wanted, he generally got.

Although she had filed for divorce, Rita was still pining for Orson Welles. Hopes of a reunion were uppermost in her mind when she and Shifra booked into the Hotel du Cap in Antibes. Orson was due to visit Cannes, and on learning that Rita was close by, suggested taking her out to dinner. Rita was excited; the evening seemed to go well, and she began to believe they might be reconciled once more. But she was sadly mistaken, for Welles left for Rome shortly after their evening together without seeing or speaking to her again.

Riviera romance

Broken-hearted, Rita was in no mood to enjoy herself. So when Elsa Maxwell rang her with an invitation to dinner, she was not enthusiastic. 'I'm in all this trouble about Orson and I can't

🌀 *During Rita and Aly's tour around Spain in the summer of 1948, the couple stopped in Seville to see the city of her father's birth and to visit Cansino relatives – especially her grandfather, old 'Padre' Cansino left. Padre, the founder of the family's traditional dancing school, had himself returned to Seville for a visit. As a child, Rita had met Padre during his stay with her family in the US when grandfather and granddaughter spent most of their time together sitting on the porch while he carved castanets for her. Although they talked little at that time, Padre was to be Rita's special favourite until his death in 1954*

Aly had to leave France on business in his plane, 'The Avenger'. But he had no intention of allowing Rita to forget him for a moment. Armfuls of red roses arrived every morning, until Rita's suite resembled a florist's shop. He telephoned her constantly, and upon his return to France began his campaign in earnest, inviting her to dinner in intimate restaurants and taking her dancing. But still Rita fought shy of getting involved with the playboy Prince.

A destiny foretold

She even went into hiding to avoid his attentions. Rita and her secretary/companion Shifra left for the nearby small town of Beaulieu-sur-Mer, where they planned to lie low until Aly gave up his hot pursuit. Here, Rita had her fortune told by an Italian gypsy woman. The gypsy told her that a man she already knew, and whom she had been resisting, would bring her great happiness. She must change her mind, or she would always regret it.

think of parties,' she said. But Elsa was nothing if not persuasive, and Rita was used to being told what to do. Advising her to buy a new white dress – in which she should arrive dramatically late – Elsa told her, 'I want you to meet a Persian prince … a wonderful person, and he will amuse you and entertain you…. You'll forget your troubles for an evening.' And so she agreed.

Rita's radiant appearance that night did not reflect her fragile state of health, nor her emotional turmoil. When she arrived, late as suggested, the assembled guests gasped with admiration. Prince Aly Khan was immediately smitten, and thrilled to be sitting next to Rita at dinner. It seemed as if all his fantasies had come true – indeed, he was so taken with her he postponed an important trip to Ireland to watch one of his beloved horses take part in a race.

Weaving a spell

After dinner that night, Aly drove Rita up into the hills above Cannes. Always romantic, he wanted her to see the stars. For Aly, it was love at first sight. He felt as if he was walking on air, he confided to his chauffeur. He invited her to his house, the Château de l'Horizon, for the following afternoon. When Rita arrived, three hours late, everything had been carefully prepared. The Prince had bought some dance music specially, for he longed to dance with Rita and hold her close. The afternoon went well, although Rita, aware of the Prince's dubious reputation with women, was resisting getting involved.

WORTH HIS WEIGHT IN DIAMONDS

1946 was the year of the Aga Khan's Diamond Jubilee. A spectacular celebration in Bombay was organized by Aly Khan, to reaffirm his father's position within the Ismaili sect in the post-war world. Following tradition, the Aga was to be publicly weighed – this time, against diamonds.

As the crowd watched, the portly Aga, arrayed in a white silk robe and blue turban, mounted his throne, which was balanced on an enormous set of scales. Eighty boxes of diamonds – offerings from his followers – were stacked up on the other side of the scales: the Aga Khan weighed in at 243 pounds, equivalent to £640,000 worth of diamonds. When he announced that all the money was to go into a Diamond Jubilee Trust Fund, his followers were overwhelmed with excitement. The theatrical ceremony had paid off and he was undeniably popular once more

Popperfoto

Totally convinced by the fortune-teller, Rita at once decided to return to Antibes. Within a short time she had moved into the three-storey Château with Aly, and the gossip-hungry tongues of the Riviera began to wag in earnest. One month after they first met, Rita and Aly set off for a two-week holiday in nearby Spain. Aly, recklessly driving a brand-new Cadillac, had unrealistic hopes of avoiding the attentions of the press. They booked into separate suites at the Ritz in Madrid, but the Spanish newspapers were one jump ahead of the couple and soon they were forced to leave for Toledo. Peace and quiet eluded them. Wild crowds chanted their names at the bullfight they unwisely attended. Rita was terrified, for they had nearly caused a riot.

There were a few happy moments in Seville, however, when Rita and Aly entertained some of Rita's Spanish relatives. After dinner in a pretty outdoor restaurant, Rita and her old grandfather, Padre Cansino, took the floor. Rita's abandoned flamenco dancing electrified the Prince; mesmerized by her flowing red hair and swirling skirts, he made up his mind to marry her. As soon as he was divorced, of course.

American interlude

Rita, still uncertain of Aly, had to return to America for professional reasons. Before she left, she tried to break off the affair – but Aly was not easily dissuaded. He followed her to Hollywood and rented a furnished house opposite Rita's. The Prince continued to woo her with thoughtfulness and charm. He played for hours with her three-year-old daughter, Rebecca, bought Shifra an expensive watch, and indulged Rita in her desire to stay quietly and simply at home.

Hoping for a romantic break, the couple

Days before their wedding, Rita and Aly were mobbed by a curious crowd while they attempted to view an art exhibition at the United States Art Gallery in Cannes above. This was a trying time for Rita. She had hoped that by announcing her forthcoming marriage to Aly, she would be able to find some peace with her fiancé and end the scandal and the constant press attention that her private life had been attracting. Instead, she found that she would have to put up with Aly's ever-present house guests at the Cannes château and, in addition, conceal her unexpected pregnancy from the prying public eye

'Aly was her great escape from Hollywood'

ORSON ON RITA

took a disastrous trip to Mexico City where their hotel was besieged by reporters. Many of the press infiltrated the hotel disguised as maids, waiters and lift attendants. The couple left for Acapulco, on the coast, and managed to snatch a few peaceful days together. Finally, after a stressful interlude in Havana, they returned to Hollywood. It seemed as if Aly had overcome Rita's resistance at last.

Rita's divorce was finalized, she cancelled her next film project, closed up her house and dismissed the servants. She was in love with Aly; his kindness, charm and passionate love for her seemed genuine at last. Rita, Aly, little Rebecca and Shifra boarded the *Britannic* on 15 December 1948. They were sailing for Ireland where they planned to spend a quiet Christmas at Aly's Gilltown stud. Back in Hollywood, a spokesman for Columbia Studios issued a statement: 'At the moment there is no question of

AP/Topham

THE MATCHMAKER

Elsa Maxwell was a Hollywood columnist and the undisputed social arbiter of the Hollywood crowd who descended on the fashionable South of France in 1948. Outside Cannes, in the little village of Auribeau, Elsa regularly hosted lavish dinner parties for distinguished guests. It was at one of these evenings that Elsa had arranged for Aly and Rita to meet. And although Rita had originally attempted to turn down the invitation, Elsa had persuaded her to change her mind and even instructed her on what to wear for the occasion and when to arrive. The matchmaking, was, of course, a success. Elsa is pictured with Rita at the Grand Prix de Paris at Longchamp *above* after Rita's marriage to Aly

matrimony. Rita is fond of Aly, and he is of her, but he is a married man. Aly has time to be attentive. Rita likes to be entertained.' But the scandal continued to grow unchecked.

By the beginning of 1949, while Rita and Aly were celebrating the new year in Switzerland, the newspapers began to adopt a more critical attitude. Headlines such as 'This Affair is an Insult to all Decent Women' and 'A Very Sordid Business' drew readers' attention to articles which questioned Rita's morality, and cast doubts upon her fitness as a mother. Moral outrage rapidly escalated in the US, where sermons were preached decrying Rita's behaviour. The American Federation of Women's Clubs were all for boycotting her films, and even the trade magazine *The Hollywood Reporter* suggested that the industry 'wash its hands of Rita Hayworth'.

Gossip and scandal

This bad publicity worried Aly, too. Although the Aga Khan had been a great lover of women in his day, it had been much easier to be discreet about his affairs. Aly was his son, and would one day inherit his position as spiritual leader. And yet here was his heir forever surrounded by a cloud of sexual gossip and scandal. This, he knew, damaged the whole family and undermined his own position.

Consequently, the Aga Khan sent his fourth wife, Yvette, to Gstaad to remonstrate with the couple. There was little choice, as he saw it. Either they break up immediately, or marry. Rita, accompanied by Aly, left for France, where the ailing Aga Khan waited to see them.

AP/Wide World Photos

Kobal Collection

♛ *Aly and Rita are photographed together during their brief stay in Switzerland* above. *It was at this time that the couple was continuously dogged by the press. Rita was dubbed an immoral woman and the constant mention of Aly's name in connection with these affairs angered his father, the Aga. To suppress the outcry, Aly had to make the decision to marry Rita as soon as possible*

♛ Left *The night before they were secretly to board the ship for Europe, Rita and Aly spent an evening at a New York nightclub with film stars Mary Pickford and Buddy Rogers*

Popperfoto

Columbia/Kobal Collection

♛ A blonde Rita wore this feminine gown *left* for her role in Orson Welles's film, *Lady from Shanghai*. Lengths of translucent white fabric form a fitted strapless bodice and fall into a flowing full-length skirt that is touched with diamanté

♛ A sophisticated emerald-patterned dress was worn for one of Rita's many publicity stills *above*. Comprised of three separate sections – sarong skirt, fitted midriff panel and top that sweeps back over the shoulders – the dress enhances Rita's figure

♛ On her arrival in London where she filmed a portion of *A Fire Down Below*, Rita wore a flame-coloured dress with a pencil-thin skirt and a short cape top *far right*. Matching belt, bag and three strands of pearls accessorized the outfit

HOLLYWOOD GLAMOUR

Rita's wardrobe was a curious mix of her own clothes and the clothes she wore for her many film roles and publicity stills. In general, however, she is best remembered for her very feminine, figure-hugging garments and pretty, flowing frocks

♛ *Left* Rita married Prince Aly Khan in an ice-blue chiffon dress created by French designer Jacques Fath. A floppy-brimmed picture hat topped with swirls of blue fabric mirrored the volume and the gauziness of the full-skirted dress

Elbow length cape top, made in two halves and seamed together over the shoulders

Closely fitted sleeves made in two pieces, finished with turn back cuffs and trimmed with tiny buttons

Sun-ray pleated full skirt falling to just above ankle length

♛ This red sun dress *above* was worn by a young Rita for a publicity shot. It has a short, slightly flared skirt and is cinched at the waist by a matching belt with a mother-of-pearl buckle

♛ Rita wears an elasticated satin swimsuit with a peach hibiscus pattern and fagoted seams for a photo session in an imitation beach setting *right*. Her necklace is made of pottery sea horses strung on a rubberized cord

♛ Royal blue silk jersey pyjama bottoms and matching short-sleeved bolero *right* were worn by Rita for a publicity still before the release of a film she made for MGM. Beneath the bolero she wears a cross-over draped bodice, which is short enough to expose a bit of midriff

Jersey silk bolero with short puff sleeves

Effective use of stripes for this boned and darted strapless peach top

Voluminous pajama trousers gathered into narrow waistband

Fitted shorts darted and seamed, with turn-ups

♛ Rita's playsuit *right* is a combination of green tailored shorts and a green and white striped bodice which is shaped with whalebone and trimmed with a strip of the same green material used for the shorts

Lynne Robinson

WEDDING EXTRAVAGANZA

MASTERMINDED BY ALY, THE WEDDING PARTY WAS A HUGE CELEBRATION OF THE MARRIAGE OF TWO OF THE WORLD'S MOST GLAMOROUS PEOPLE. RITA, SURROUNDED BY STRANGERS, FOUND IT AN INTOLERABLE STRAIN

Popperfoto

♔ *Below The Villa Yakimour where the Aga Khan lived, about four miles from Aly's Château de l'Horizon. Aly had to go to the Villa for a tense meeting with his father immediately after the long drive from Switzerland to Cannes, but first he dropped Rita at the château, where she tried to get some rest and nerve herself for her own audience with the Aga Khan. She knew that everything depended upon the impression she made on the old man; if he withheld his consent to their marriage, she and Aly would have to break off their relationship altogether*

♔ *The weeks leading up to the announcement of the wedding were a terrible strain for the four people most closely concerned. Luckily, Rita and the Aga Khan took an instant liking to each other and when he had given his blessing to the marriage, Rita and the family could smile happily for the press photographers at the Villa Yakimour above. Rita sits centre between the Aga Khan left and the Begum right. Aly stands behind his bride-to-be*

ILLA YAKIMOUR HAD 21 ROOMS AND WAS situated in a quiet suburb of Cannes. Here the Aga Khan, now 72, spent long hours lying on a *chaise-longue* in the 'salon', dictating letters, reading newspapers and keeping control of his empire. By the time Rita and Aly arrived, he was deeply concerned about his son's reputation. He spent 15 minutes alone with the Prince, and then it was Rita's turn to face the powerful old man.

She was feeling unwell, a combination of nerves and flu. It seemed as if her whole future hung on this highly charged meeting. The Aga had been expecting the worst, but he still had an eye for a beautiful woman – and when he saw Rita his anger and doubt soon melted away. 'I know of no-one who is more quiet or lady-like,' he told the press later. Rita, too, was charmed and, holding his hand, told him that he was 'very sweet'. Once he realized how devoted the couple were, he advised them 'to get married as soon as possible'.

Rita and Aly's love affair had fuelled a frenzy of salacious gossip, whipped up by the world's press. Now, with the public announcement of their wedding, the media's attitude was transformed – although inquisitive pressure still mounted.

'I hope that my private affairs will be treated with the consideration which is usually extended to the private affairs of individuals in general,' pleaded the Prince, but reporters from all over the world continued to monitor the couple's every move. It was like a fairy-tale; Aly was dubbed the Prince of Love, or Prince Charming, while Rita – already a fantasy figure – became Cinderella, marrying her Prince against all odds.

Aly's family rallied round. The press were invited to a photo-session at the Villa Yakimour during which the Aga Khan, his Begum in a jewelled sari, and the happy couple posed for pictures. 'There are 150,000 divorces in Britain annually,' said the Aga. 'Why should everyone criticize my son?'

Secret rendezvous

As the pressures mounted, Rita began to panic. Had she made a big mistake? She was horrified by Aly's gregarious nature; the Château de

Popperfoto

l'Horizon was always full of guests, many of whom the Prince barely knew. She was certain, too, that some of the glamorous women who stayed there had been Aly's mistresses. Her feelings of jealousy and insecurity fuelled the nagging doubts she was beginning to have about her future with Aly.

Rita made an extraordinary decision. She sent Orson Welles a telegram, asking him to meet her at a hotel in Antibes. He responded immediately, and made the journey standing up in a cargo plane as he couldn't get a seat. Rita had prepared a romantic setting. There were candles, and champagne on ice. Knowing her ex-husband's fondness for pretty lingerie, she was dressed in a filmy, feminine négligé. Welles was astonished, and even more so when she said, 'Here I am. Marry me.'

He refused her offer; he cared for her very much, but was in love with someone else at the time. Rita had to go back to Aly as if nothing had happened.

Despite the crowds of reporters and gaggles of curious tourists outside the château, Aly

♛ Above *At last the announcement had been made. The newspapers were filled with photographs of Rita and Aly and the couple hoped that, now they were officially engaged, the constant hounding and prurient speculation would cease. But an air of scandal still hovered over them. Legally, Aly was still married to Joan and the divorce could not be granted until a French judge had tried to reconcile the married couple and talk Rita and Aly out of their proposed wedding. Then, in March 1949, Rita became pregnant and the couple had something new to keep from the hordes of reporters who still dogged their every move*

AP/Topham

and Rita continued to hope for a simple and intimate ceremony. Accordingly, Aly applied to the French Ministry of Justice for permission to hold a civil ceremony at home.

Under French law, a marriage must be performed in public at a *mairie*, or town hall. Concern for his father's health, which had not been good, and fears of being inundated with jostling hordes of journalists and bystanders, were uppermost in Aly's mind. An additional question mark hung over the actual date of the ceremony, for his divorce from Joan was not yet finalized. Invitations were printed, but the date was left tantalizingly blank.

Eventually, Aly's gambling instincts took over and, although he was still officially married and had not heard from the Ministry of Justice, they set the date: 27 May 1949. There were to be about 100 'close friends' present, plus a selection of journalists.

The guest list was an exotic blend of royalty, high society and show-business people. It boasted a maharajah and maharanee, an emir, seven princes, four princesses, couturier Jacques Fath, artist Maurice Utrillo, singer Edith Piaf and her sometime lover and protégé Yves Montand. Rita's own contribution hinted at her innate shyness and sad lack of true friendship. She invited a meagre number, of whom only six turned up. These included her business manager, press agent and personal agent.

An ordeal for Rita

Aly began to plan the reception with typical enthusiasm and energy. He masterminded not only the party itself, but organized pre-wedding entertainment for the days leading up to the sparkling event. Rita's most recent film, *The Loves of Carmen*, was shown in a privately rented theatre to just about everyone — including servants, tradesmen, and the caterers who were preparing the wedding lunch.

This was a terrible ordeal for Rita, who was feeling tired because she was pregnant. When she left the cinema, she had to fight her way through the inevitable large crowd that had gathered outside. They were so desperate for a close look at the film star that they forced open the door of her limousine. Excited fans ran after the car until it sped out of reach.

A public event

The couple's wish for a private ceremony was not to be granted. Just 48 hours before their wedding day, they were refused permission to hold the ceremony at the château. On hearing the news, Rita burst into tears, for she had a genuine fear of unruly crowds.

But nothing could be done. The contingency plan — to marry at the little town hall in the hills at Vallauris — was put into action. Aly

had received his divorce barely a month before the wedding date; his restless tendency to live close to the edge certainly pervaded his romance and marriage to Rita.

Paul Derigon, the Communist Mayor of Vallauris, was delighted. What a *coup* for the sleepy, sunbaked town where Picasso had worked as a potter but little else had ever happened. With admirable speed he borrowed a red carpet, tapestries, flowers, and had the largest room in the town hall freshly painted.

> **' ... it was a passion, but passion is part of love and he loved Rita very much'**
>
> ALY'S MATERNAL UNCLE

The Prince donated one million francs cash, eccentrically wrapped up in a newspaper, to the little town's treasury — and begged the Mayor to restrict the numbers of journalists. Indeed, he was so worried about the press that he even arrived at the *mairie* an hour before his wedding in an unsuccessful attempt to have the waiting reporters excluded from the inevitably public ceremony.

Popperfoto

⬙ Above *Final touches: American, French and British flags are put over the door of the* mairie *at Vallauris. They had asked permission for a private ceremony but, according to French law, the protest of a single individual was enough to force the couple to get married in public. That individual was actually an astute French journalist who wished to attend the ceremony. Now the entire press corps could crash what should have been a private celebration. Early that morning, Aly pleaded with Mayor Derigon to exclude the reporters and photographers from the ceremony. Briefly, he succeeded, and the mayor ordered 75 furious journalists out of the room*

⬙ Right *Elegant and bravely smiling in spite of her fear of crowds, Rita leaves her white Cadillac convertible and pauses a moment for the photographers before entering the* mairie. *Once inside, she and Aly could clearly hear the argument raging between Mayor Derigon and the ousted reporters. Eventually, Derigon gave in and the press filed noisily and angrily back into the room*

Syndication International

Popperfoto

ALY'S ART COLLECTION

In the post-war years, Aly – with the help of a knowledgeable Nice-based art dealer – began to build a notable collection of paintings. Many were by French Impressionists such as Utrillo, but Aly was especially fond of work by Raoul Dufy and bought many of his scenes of London and of racecourses. Boudin, too, was well represented; perhaps his views of Trouville brought back memories of Aly's childhood holidays on the Normandy coast.

Sadly, Aly was forced to sell the collection in 1957 when crippling debts – largely caused by his gambling – became too pressing. Not even the son of the fabulously wealthy Aga Khan could live on credit forever. At a large sale at Galerie Charpentier in Paris, attended by a fashionable crowd, many of the paintings were bought by the film magnate Mike Todd honeymooning with his new wife, Elizabeth Taylor

♛ **Left** *Prince Aly Khan arrives at the town hall about an hour before the wedding ceremony. Exhausted, tense and still battling for privacy, he managed to maintain his composure even when accosted on the steps by yet another reporter. Derigon had agreed to conduct the ceremony on the ground floor, in order to save the old Aga Khan from trudging upstairs, but insisted upon throwing open the doors of the room to allow anyone who so wished to enter*

♛ **Below** *The famous kiss. Prince Aly Khan kissed his bride on the mouth, an American custom which caused quite a few raised eyebrows among the French onlookers. Mayor Derigon (far right) then made his speech, prefacing it with the words 'Your Highnesses' – the first time Rita had ever heard herself addressed this way. French civil ceremonies are very brief and, just eight minutes after the wedding had begun, Rita found herself out in the sunlight again, a Princess about to embark on a life quite different from anything she had ever known*

that he was in the presence of royalty, hesitantly asked them if they accepted each other as husband and wife. '*Oui, oui*,' said Rita, quietly. '*Oui, oui*,' affirmed Aly, and they exchanged wedding rings. The register was duly signed by the couple and their witnesses.

They were man and wife, Prince and Princess. Aly slid his arm around Rita's waist and kissed her so passionately on the lips that some of those present were slightly shocked.

27 May was a beautiful, sunny Mediterranean day. An exhausted, tense Aly waited for his bride inside the *mairie*. He was conventionally dressed in an English morning suit. Outside, the excited mêlée of reporters, photographers, policemen and onlookers were estimated to number more than a thousand.

Happy applause greeted the arrival of the Aga Khan and his Begum – who arrived punctually at 11.00am. They emerged from a green Rolls-Royce, the Begum elegant and stately in a pale blue sari, the Aga dressed for hot weather in a cream suit and sunglasses. He smiled bravely and waved cheerfully to the crowds.

As the numbers swelled to some 3000 spectators, a gleaming white Cadillac convertible, complete with impressive police escort, drew up. Inside, a nervous Rita Hayworth listened to the encouraging cheers as the crowds called her name. She was wearing an ice-blue chiffon dress with a matching large-brimmed hat by Jacques Fath. Girlishly, she waved a small white handkerchief as she posed with Mayor Derigon on the town hall steps.

Rita and Aly, seated in the French tradition, listened as their marriage licence was solemnly read out. Then the Mayor, suddenly conscious

AP/Wide World Photos

Popperfoto

into the ivy which clung to the château walls.

The food and drink were no less lavish. One of the Riviera's star chefs had been hired to prepare the luncheon, and prodigious quantities of luxury foods had been ordered. These included 40 lobsters, 10 pounds of caviar and an enormous 120-pound wedding cake.

A new cocktail, named the Ritaly, was specially created for the occasion. This heady mixture consisted of two-thirds whisky, one-third vermouth, two drops of bitters and a cherry. Over 400 were drunk that day – mainly, according to the chief barman, by journalists.

While the Aga Khan nervously consumed startling amounts of caviar, a bemused Rita sat in an armchair surrounded by Indian guests. Each one knelt before their new Princess, kissed her foot, and presented her with a gift. The Aga was later to comment that it 'was a fantastic, semi-royal, semi-Hollywood affair; my wife and I played our part in the ceremony, much as we disapproved of the atmosphere with which it was surrounded.'

A sober ceremony

The following day, two white-robed mullahs from the Paris mosque conducted a quiet and serious Islamic ceremony attended by colourfully dressed Ismaili nobles from all over the

But the wedding party applauded and settled back to listen to the Mayor's carefully prepared speech of thanks and flowery wishes to the royal couple for their future together.

Aly was restless, Rita silent, as Derigon spoke of the great honour they had done his humble little town. Finally, he concluded: 'I wish with all my heart, and a sincere hope that after the feverish days you have been experiencing, which are the price of glory and success, that you may find in this oasis the happiness that you desire in calm and tranquillity. Prince, Princess, our dearest wish is that you may be happy in our community.'

As the Prince and his glamorous Princess left the town hall, they were showered with rice, photographed yet again, and cheered wildly. With visible relief, they got into the open Cadillac and drove the two miles to the château. The couple relaxed sufficiently to smile and wave at the groups of well-wishers who lined the route. It had all gone well.

The reception

Back at the château, everything was extravagantly prepared. The swimming-pool had been filled in true oriental fashion with 200 gallons of eau-de-Cologne. Floating upon its scented surface were two 12ft-long letters formed out of white carnations: M for Margarita and A for Aly. Thousands more flowers had been wired

♛ **Above** *Legally joined at last, the lovers, half-blinded by flash bulbs, drive away from the ceremony in Aly's white convertible and the Prince relaxes into his first smile of the day. Motorcycle police escorted them to the Château de l'Horizon where buffet tables piled high with delicacies awaited the guests*

♛ *The dazzling new Princess, outshining even the 12-carat diamond on her left hand, touched off the celebrations by cutting the wedding cake right under her husband's proud gaze, and the glittering party began. Yves Montand sang to the guests on the upper terrace while the reporters, penned into the lower terrace top right, clustered around Jules's bar and drank quantities of his new Ritaly cocktail. The festivities lasted some six hours and at length the weary bride joined her father-in-law at the centre table. The old man seemed fatigued himself and was heard to say, 'Too much caviar, Rita. Too much caviar'*

AP/Wide World Photos

world. Aly promised his bride a house and a dowry, parts of the Koran were read out and, this time, the couple were toasted in fruit juice – as befitted Islamic law.

Almost immediately, Aly left the house and went out, leaving his pregnant and exhausted bride to rest, alone. He seemed desperate for some time to himself, and was already feeling restricted. Indeed, Aly had never really changed. During the preparations for their wedding, he had cleverly evaded reporters by slipping out of the château in the early hours of the morning. On one such expedition – to Cannes Casino – he had offered Rita's business manager, Lee Ellroy, a choice of two attractive women. Ellroy was not interested, but Aly disappeared with one of the girls.

An attempt to explain Aly's behaviour was made by a close friend: 'Aly was a tender man and a sentimental man, with an enormous affection for Rita. But he was of Oriental origin and to him it was of no great importance to "pillage" a little. To see a woman on the side was of no importance at all.' And, as his own maternal uncle said, 'With Aly, it was not that kind of strong love which lasts; it was perhaps superficial, it was a passion, but passion is part of love and he loved Rita very much. And Rita, surely she was in love with Aly.'

Popperfoto

THE CHATEAU DE L'HORIZON

Aly bought the Château de l'Horizon on the French Riviera in the late 1940s when it cost him about £30,000. Built for an American actress before World War 2, it was not a grand house, but its stylishness appealed to Aly. The site was superb and it soon became a favourite place for the Prince to entertain fashionable friends and acquaintances

♛ The living room *below* was, above all, a place of comfort, with sofas and armchairs upholstered in beige linen and an ornately patterned carpet in front of the fireplace. French doors led out from this room onto the terrace that overlooked the swimming pool

♛ Limited in extent because of the site, the grounds *below centre* were carefully designed to provide maximum interest for pathways by means of dramatic sculpture and a well-chosen variety of shrubs, trees and flowers. Maintenance was kept to a minimum

♛ The château *left* was designed by Barry Dierks for American actress Maxine Elliott. Its modern appearance and spaciousness – there were ten bedrooms and seven bathrooms – together with its site and location, close to Cannes, appealed at once to Aly. Sunlight flooded in through the large windows, adding to the open, informal atmosphere. The lower terrace gave access to a chute that led down to the sea. One of the bedrooms was named after Winston Churchill, who stayed here briefly during World War 2

♛ Nestling in the verdant hills overlooking the Mediterranean, the château was split into several levels. The swimming pool dominated the lower level *below,* while the terrace above it was where buffet lunches were served to guests almost daily. But the globetrotting Prince usually spent no more than three months of the year at the château

AP/Wide World Photos

A MARRIAGE DISINTEGRATES

RITA'S NEW ROLE AS PRINCESS ALY KHAN PROVED TO BE QUITE BEYOND HER – ALL SHE CRAVED WAS A QUIET LIFE AT HOME, WHILE ALY WANTED A HIGH-PROFILE, GLAMOROUS WIFE

♛ Though passionately in love, neither Aly nor Rita seemed able to adapt to the other's lifestyle. Aly was happiest surrounded by people – constantly on the move, he went to many of Europe's great social events and enjoyed horse races such as the Derby, where they celebrated their first wedding anniversary below. Rita, despite her glamorous image, preferred to spend quiet, intimate evenings with her husband above right

RITA'S DREAMS OF BLISSFUL DOMESTICITY were never to come true. Aly liked to live surrounded by people, while his restless spirit required constant entertainment and stimulation. Their early married life soon settled into an uneasy pattern as both tried to retain their separate and preferred way of life.

While Aly went out, night after night, Rita stayed quietly at home. She had let her hair return to its natural colour, wore jeans and used very little make-up. She loved to sleep late, and enjoyed a large breakfast of ham and eggs, orange juice and coffee on the terrace. There were sad evenings when, all alone in her bedroom, she would dance to the Spanish music of her childhood. And there were scenes, arguments and periods of sulking.

Rita was also finding her new role as Princess Aly Khan remarkably hard to master. A

Hulton Picture Company

Georgian prince was brought in to instruct her in all manner of delicate points of etiquette. In addition, she was struggling to learn French. She tried hard to please Aly. 'It was too difficult for me,' she said later. 'I wasn't prepared for it and, who knows, he probably wasn't prepared for me.'

Socially, too, she was completely out of her depth. Aly mixed with a very sophisticated international group of people. Rita, having trouble with the language, and overwhelmed by his friends, still accompanied Aly to numerous social and sporting events. Her pregnancy a secret, Rita found crowds more of a strain than ever. She fainted in public on two occasions – at Longchamps race track in Paris, and at the Festival of Stars in the Tuileries Gardens. That August, the couple confirmed all the rumours about Rita's pregnancy and announced that the baby was due in February – but not that Rita was, in fact, five months pregnant already.

Deauville days

As he had done every summer since he was a small boy, Aly chose to spend August in Deauville. Rita wore specially designed maternity clothes in public now, and seemed to relax a little. Their hectic social life continued, although Rita would often retire to bed very early while Aly went out gambling.

In the afternoons, Aly would play happily with the children – Rebecca and his two sons – on the sandy beach in front of the Villa Gorizia. Rita was then at her happiest and most content. Barefoot, she would join in their games. But underneath such deceptive scenes lay a darker pattern. 'He was like quicksilver that summer,' said one friend. 'He'd disappear in the

morning to see the horses … come back for breakfast and disappear again. Suddenly Rita would find that 25 people had been invited to lunch. There would be six women there we all suspected Aly had been sleeping with. Everyone was watching her.' Rita tried to ignore Aly's philandering, perhaps hoping, perhaps believing, that the birth of their child would cement the marriage. What else could she do?

A family at last

As the time drew near, Rita and Aly flew to Switzerland to await the birth. They took a large suite in the Lausanne Palace Hotel, and reserved an equally luxurious one for Rita at the Montchoisi Clinic, one of the most prestigious clinics in Europe. The couple were not the only ones who were waiting; the press were speculating wildly too. Aly and Rita were still publicly sticking to February, although there had been various allusions to 'premature' babies running in the family.

Aly was on his best and most solicitous behaviour. He bought Rita flowers, chocolates and other presents almost every day and took her for a drive in his Cadillac each afternoon. Rita was tired and strained, and there was some concern for her health. However, at 9.45 in the

♛ *Some of Rita's happiest times with Aly were spent quietly in Switzerland awaiting the arrival of their baby* below. *She dreamed of having a 'normal' family life but this was not to be fulfilled*

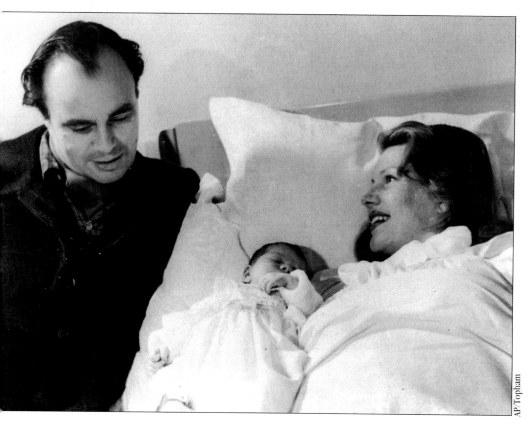

AP/Topham

spotted out on the town with an American dancer whose new diamond necklace was rumoured to be a gift from the Prince.

An anniversary incident

Rita and Aly celebrated their first wedding anniversary at the Derby. Their marriage was tempestuous, yet every row was followed by a romantic reconciliation. But Rita's growing disenchantment with her husband was highlighted by an incident in Paris in June 1950. Orson Welles was appearing in two short plays and Rita very much wanted to attend the première with her new husband. Perhaps she wanted some kind of revenge, for she had not seen Orson since her last-minute marriage proposal in Antibes.

Rita, dressed in black lace with diamond combs in her wavy hair, looked particularly lovely that night. She and Aly sat in the third row, hidden behind a woman in a flamboyant feathered hat. Fortunately for Rita's plans, the woman did not return to her seat after the break. During the second part of the show, Orson had a tremendous shock when he spotted his ex-wife, diamond earrings glittering, gazing up from the audience. His reaction must have been everything Rita had hoped for and more. She laughed merrily, and must have been pleased when Aly reacted by sulking jealously for the remainder of their strange evening.

While in Paris, Aly came to the conclusion that Rita should go back to work. Aware of his wife's resistance, he took matters into his own hands and chartered Errol Flynn's yacht, *La Zaca*, for a holiday. One of the guests was to be Charles Vidor, Rita's old director. Despite Rita's unpredictable moods and dislike of sailing, she enjoyed talking with him, seeming amenable to the idea of working once again. She also needed some money, since Aly was

morning, on 28 December 1949, Rita safely gave birth to a 5lb 8oz baby girl. Her name was to be Yasmin. 'I told you,' quipped the Prince to reporters. 'Premature babies run in our family.'

A delighted Aly filled Rita's room with fresh lilac blooms, and seemed transformed by the birth of his third child. In the three months that followed he appeared to have abandoned his old habits; they rented a comfortable chalet in Gstaad and enjoyed all their children, including the baby Princess. 'This was the happiest time of our life together,' said Rita. 'It was the one time we were a family.'

Aly seeks diversion

This peaceful episode ended abruptly when Aly broke his leg in a skiing accident. As soon as the doctors agreed, Aly left the hospital and the entire family flew back to the South of France. With his leg in a large plaster cast, Aly was bored and searched for entertainment. Streams of visitors arrived to play cards and chat to the injured Prince.

Needless to say, many of these visitors were beautiful women, and Rita's jealousy and anger were soon roused once more. There were terrible scenes in which Rita's fiery Latin temper burst out of control. Aly, however, was unstoppable, and did not allow his wife's blazing temper to prevent him enjoying himself. Complete with plaster cast and crutches, Aly left the château for Paris. He had a genuine reason for the trip: he was buying a new house there. Nevertheless, he was soon

👑 *Aly was delighted when Yasmin was born on 28 December 1949 in Lausanne above. He showered Rita with gifts and for a few months they seemed an idyllic family. Even his father, the Aga Khan below, approved of his new granddaughter. Now Rita thought she could have the security of close family life, but Aly quickly became bored: when an accident prevented further skiing, he insisted that the family move to the South of France where he could find friends willing to entertain him*

UPI/Bettmann Newsphotos

THE HOLLYWOOD WITCH HUNTS

As the dust began to settle in post-war Europe, a new 'enemy' reared its head. Communism would, it was claimed, split the world apart and ruin any chance of long-term peace. This hysteria was particularly rampant in the American film industry which, since it promoted ideas through stories, was imagined to be especially vulnerable to left-wing infiltration.

In 1947 the Committee on Un-American Activities was set up to expose Communists and to eradicate any left-wing content from Hollywood films. Between 1950 and 1954 this organization hounded – and in some cases destroyed – many individuals working in the film industry. Hollywood was almost at war with itself as film stars took sides and paranoia mounted. One of those who firmly allied themselves with

the right wing was an actor called Ronald Reagan, while *below* Humphrey Bogart, Lauren Bacall and Danny Kaye were among a group of film notables protesting the Committee's activities.

Rita Hayworth was caught up in this hysteria too, although she escaped comparatively lightly. In 1951 the FBI informed her studio, Columbia, that she had been involved with some suspiciously left-wing political organizations. These links dated from the time of her marriage to Orson Welles. In truth, Rita was not a politically committed person. She had lent her name and glamorous image to various associations simply to please Orson. Eventually, Rita was forced to sign a statement affirming that she had never been a member of the Communist Party and that she was a loyal citizen of the USA

Popperfoto

'It was too difficult for me . . .'

RITA ON LIFE WITH ALY

Popperfoto

🕮 *Despite their dazzling lifestyle, Aly and Rita were often short of money. In order to persuade Rita to return to work in Hollywood, Aly arranged a cruising party on La Zaca, Errol Flynn's yacht above. The yacht's luxurious fittings included a bedroom whose walls and ceiling were completely lined with mirrors*

still on an allowance from his father, and his extravagant way of life meant that they were often short of cash.

African tour

Aly was pleased that Rita might work again; after all, he had married a film star and to a certain extent enjoyed basking in reflected glory. But first he wanted her to accompany him on a tour of Ismaili communities in Africa.

The African visit was to be extensive, for there were many Ismailis scattered through several countries. Aly invited two of Rita's friends along to help her relax, since he realized how scared she was of appearing in public as the official wife of a religious leader.

The Prince contacted Columbia Studios and asked them to stop issuing any more pin-up pictures of his wife – for the time being,

anyway. Although most of his followers were perfectly happy with his marriage, Aly could not afford to take any unnecessary risks. They left for Cairo, where Rita's friends joined them in the inevitable socializing. Aly was enjoying catching up with many friends.

He was in his element on New Year's Eve at a candlelit party given by an old Polish girlfriend. Rita was miserable, and sat alone in the darkened room while Aly flitted from one group to the next. Suddenly, she rose and left without saying goodbye. A worried Aly followed her, looking – according to the hostess – 'rather unhappy'.

Nairobi was the next stop on their itinerary. Arriving in a tiny aeroplane, they were greeted by crowds of ecstatic followers. Rita was photographed, flowers were pressed into her hands, and garlands of welcome hung

Topham

🜲 *Being a 'married bachelor' – separated but not divorced – seemed to suit Aly. With Rita back in Hollywood, he was free to escort as many beautiful women as he wanted – for instance, Joan Fontaine above – without giving them any expectations of marrying him*

about her neck. To please Aly, she managed to hide her genuine terror and carry on.

There were many public events to attend. Aly had to perform marriage ceremonies and visit the Aga Khan Girls' School where they were entertained with home-made cakes and serenaded by a band of children. Unable to understand the language, Rita stood confused at countless receptions where the Ismaili women discussed their new Princess. Rita was suffering from the heat, but was not allowed to go swimming for fear of breaking strict protocol.

Aly, however, went out gambling and playing bridge with friends. Rita continued to resist his suggestion that she resume her film career; she had been working all her life and really wanted a rest. But life as the Princess Aly Khan was proving to be just as exhausting as any film role.

A safari had been planned to relieve the pressures of their trip, but they had already been away for three months and Rita was missing her children. Nor could she face the thought of yet more travelling. She told Aly that she was tired and unwell – he had better go on without her. Then she sent him a note, informing him that she was returning to France im-

mediately. Aly rushed back to Nairobi and, hoping to save face, accompanied his wife and her friends to the airport. He had further official visits to perform throughout Africa.

Flight and separation

Confused and unhappy, Rita decided to take her daughters back to the United States. She was secretly terrified that Aly – or his father – would try to take Yasmin away from her. So on the day the Aga returned to the château from Pakistan, looking forward to seeing his granddaughter, Rita and the children fled. Attempting to conceal their departure, Rita used a false name, among other ruses, to avoid pursuit.

In reality, the Aga Khan knew all about it, for the French authorities had informed both him and Aly. However, they wanted to avoid yet another scandal and believed it might be possible to persuade Rita quietly to return. 'We're travelling people,' Aly said to the press, as he tried to pretend everything was fine. He stayed in Europe while Rita languished in New York, hoping, it seemed, to be pursued. Instead, she received a letter.

'My Darling One,' he began, and went on to say, 'I am terribly sad for two reasons: first your decision, and secondly your want of confidence in me and the way you have carried it out.' He suggested a 'friendly' separation, and offered a divorce should Rita wish to remarry at any time. He requested that Yasmin be brought up in the Muslim faith, and assured Rita that she would inherit one-fifth of his property in the event of his death.

Having dealt with the business aspects, Aly added a more romantic final paragraph. 'If in time your thoughts ever turn to me and the love I have always had and have for you, my arms are then open; should such a happy change come over your wishes then the … separation … could not prevent your light returning to my life.'

When Aly deliberately 'leaked' this letter to both the French and American press, Rita was furious. She saw the whole exercise as a way of avoiding scandal and allowing Aly to become the 'married bachelor' he had been when they first met. Although Aly sent her two dozen roses on their second wedding anniversary with a note that read 'Remember me?', Rita refused to be charmed. She instructed her lawyer to begin divorce proceedings immediately, but Aly, urged on by his father, was still pressing for a reconciliation.

Return to work

Agreeing to delay proceedings by six months, Rita went back to work at Columbia. Harry Cohn was eager to make the most of all the publicity his star was attracting, while Rita herself

---

THE CHILDREN

Aly Khan was extremely fond of children and was a doting father – unlike his own rather remote parent. His two sons, Karim and Amyn, lived mostly with their mother but – like Aly himself – spent summer holidays at Deauville with their father. When Rita Hayworth left him to return to the States, he spent a fortune in legal fees to gain joint custody of Princess Yasmin, who flew to France every summer for her holidays. He showered presents on the children – and not only his own, for Rebecca Welles, Yasmin's half-sister, *seen with her right* was included in all the family treats when they were small

Robert Hunt Library

was badly in need of the money.

She began shooting *Affair in Trinidad*, a film which required her to execute some long dance sequences. She was now over 30 and no longer as fit as she had once been. 'I never had anyone at any time work harder than Rita,' said the film's choreographer afterwards.

She was having a lot of trouble with Harry Cohn, who was determined to make Rita bend to his wishes. She was so desperate that she unwisely signed a contract which gave her no script approval or control over any of her future films. 'They told me I had been away from movies for three years,' she said, 'and they didn't know if the public would accept me. I had no idea if they were right or not and I needed money. I had to do what they said.'

In pursuit of enjoyment

Aly seemed unable to play the part of a sad and lonely husband. Recklessly, he plunged into a frantic social life which attracted a good deal of publicity. One incident which appealed to the press was the time he got a black eye at Deauville. He claimed it was a sporting accident, but witnesses attested that a jealous husband had lashed out at the Prince.

Among his conquests that summer were film star Joan Fontaine and a beautiful young actress named Lise Bourdin, who was to be involved with Aly for several years.

The Aga Khan had recently suffered a heart attack. Aly flew to France when he realized how ill his father had become. More than ever before, the Aga needed his eldest son to represent his interests but he was concerned that Aly would never be mature enough for the role.

Columbia/Kobal Collection

♛ *Having been away from movie-making for over three years, Rita threw herself into work once more – from posing for publicity 'stills'* above, *to practising long and hard on difficult dance sequences*

♛ *Aly, meanwhile, continued merrily round the European social circuit, escorting the most sophisticated women. A jealous husband in Deauville was said to have given him the black eye* below

Topham

BITTER SWEET

Happy times for Rita and Aly together were few and far between: their brief marriage was dogged by misunderstanding and incompatible expectations of each other. However, the heady days of their courtship and the all too brief blissful private times they had together as a family would always serve them as poignant memories when they later looked back on their unique and sensational love affair

👑 Princess Yasmin is reunited with her father *below* after a two-year separation. Although Yasmin was caught in the centre of their divorce, she continued to be a source of joy and delight for both her adoring parents as well as a link between Rita and Aly in the years to come

UPI/Bettmann Newsphotos

UPI/Bettmann Newsphotos

👑 The early years in New York were, no doubt, the most carefree of little Margarita's life. She is shown *above* aged three with brother Eduardo Jnr. For, by the time she was four, her father had enrolled her in his brother's dance school, setting her on her long show-business career

MISS RITA HAYWORTH

AND

PRINCE ALY KHAN

INVITE YOU TO THEIR WEDDING

AT THE CHATEAU DE L'HORIZON

GOLFE JUAN

ON the 27th of May, 1949

AT 1.15 p.m.

R.S.V.P.
SECRETARY
CHATEAU DE L'HORIZON
GOLFE JUAN A.M.

👑 *Above* The wedding invitation encapsulates the difficulties, heartache and last-minute upsets which beset the couple's big day. The formal technicalities of Aly's divorce decree took so long to be completed that the wedding date had to be left blank and filled in by hand, while the venue was changed only 48 hours before the ceremony. But the trials and tribulations failed to spoil the joy the couple shared in their long-awaited nuptials

👑 *Right* Aly and Rita during an informal cruise round the Mediterranean aboard Errol Flynn's yacht *La Zaca*. Moments such as these, when the couple were alone or with a group of close friends, were among the happiest of their time together

Bettmann Archive

Kobal Collection

👑 Before his divorce from his first wife, Joan, was finalized, Aly secretly bought a huge Irish Georgian mansion *left* for his future bride, Rita. The estate – ancestral home of the Dukes of Leinster – was located close to his Gilltown stud farm in County Kildare, Ireland, and was probably meant to be an impressive home away from home for Rita and himself

Popperfoto

RECONCILIATION AND BEYOND

DESPITE THEIR DIFFERENCES, THERE WERE STILL STRONG BONDS OF LOVE BETWEEN RITA AND ALY, NOT LEAST THEIR DEVOTION TO THEIR DAUGHTER. SADLY, EFFORTS TO REGAIN THE EARLIER MAGIC FAILED. DIVORCE WAS INEVITABLE

♛ *Rita turns her back on Aly as she fields questions from the press in 1952 below. At this time the couple were estranged, so that Aly's appearance at Rita's residence in Los Angeles excited media speculation about a reconciliation. Rita, however, was non-committal*

THE AGA KHAN'S DETERIORATING HEALTH had prevented him from carrying on with his annual tour of the East. Aly loved his father, and was still in awe of him. Agreeing to take the Aga's place, he flew to India – where he tried to placate his disappointed father by working hard and keeping all his official appointments.

When he heard from his lawyers that Rita had agreed to meet him at last, Aly immediately sailed to New York. Here he intended to oversee the sale of 20 horses at the annual yearling sales in Saratoga Springs, NY. Less responsibly, he also intended to pursue his affair with the actress Yvonne De Carlo which he had begun in France. Fortunately for his other plans this remained a secret, and after a few days' dalliance the Prince flew to Los Angeles where Rita was waiting for him.

Family crisis

Aly arrived at the airport in princely style: he had 175 pounds of luggage with him, including five bulging sacks of toys for his baby daughter. It was evening by the time he reached Rita's home, and although he stayed until 2.30 in the morning, he did not spend the night there. The next day, he returned to have lunch with Rita and the children. Their reconciliation was proceeding slowly, but might never have come to anything if a near-tragic accident had not occurred that evening.

Little Princess Yasmin was found asleep at 8 pm with an empty bottle of sleeping pills on the floor beside her. Believing them to be sweets, the child seemed to have taken them all. No-one knew how many tablets were missing. Hysterical, Rita phoned Aly and told him to meet her at Santa Monica Hospital. Aly, who had just been reunited with his beloved baby girl after nearly 18 months, held Rita's hand tightly as they anxiously waited for news.

Happy together

Yasmin swiftly recovered, for when the doctors pumped her stomach they discovered that she had swallowed only a few tablets, and could be taken home that night. The intensity of the crisis had re-created a powerful emotional bond between Rita and Aly. They spent some peaceful days together which echoed those happy months in Switzerland when Yasmin was new-born. It began to look as if they could be permanently reunited, so Rita agreed to visit Aly in Paris as soon as she had finished working on the movie *Salome.*

AP/Wide World Photos

Kobal Collection

In September 1952, Rita arrived at Le Havre. Aly was not there to welcome her; instead he sent his valet. Rita hid her disappointment, but was even more upset on her arrival at their house in Paris. Aly was not there either; he had been detained on business in Cannes. She wondered how serious he was about a fresh start. The house was full of guests, too, something Aly knew Rita hated. This was not the romantic, loving reunion Rita had hoped for; hurt and puzzled, she went to bed early – and alone.

Full of ebullient charm, Aly arrived the following evening, claiming he had driven like the wind to be at her side. They spent the night together; Aly rushed out the next morning to inform the reporters, who stood waiting for news in the autumn rain. Then he left Rita 'resting' while he kept a lunch date with friends.

Despite his behaviour, and what looked like a suspiciously friendly relationship with the press, Rita agreed to announce publicly that she was not going to divorce Aly. He was triumphant. 'As far as I am concerned we have no intention of breaking up,' a smiling Aly confidently told reporters. This time it would not be another woman, or long hours at the casino, that came between Aly and Rita. It was his uncharacteristic cooperation with the press. Rita soon realized that her husband had no real intention of changing, or even compromising, his racy lifestyle. He didn't seem motivated by love at all, but sought to assuage his father's fears – and ensure his future as the next Aga.

Public squabbling

Within a short time, Rita had moved out of the house and into the Hotel Lancaster. Now it was her turn to confide in reporters. 'I love Aly very much,' she said, 'But he doesn't understand family life. He thinks only of gambling, horse racing, and big game hunting. He is a playboy, while I work all year round in Hollywood. When I come to Paris, it isn't to live in a house where there are 80 friends of all kinds coming and going ... What's more, Aly spends too much, while I have to work for the two of us.'

Tha Aga's hopes of a discreet reconciliation had been dashed. He privately advised his son to agree to a large financial settlement for Yasmin, and to put a stop to this degrading public fight. 'I thought Miss Hayworth charming and beautiful,' he wrote later, 'but it was not long

♕ Left *Rita's marriage to singer Dick Haymes in 1953 was her fourth. It proved to be a near-fatal attraction. Haymes came encumbered with a bad reputation and a host of problems, while Rita had plenty of troubles of her own. Few were surprised when the actress filed for divorce two years later*

♕ *Aly's succession of well-publicized affairs were strongly disapproved of by the Aga Khan, who felt the Prince's lifestyle reflected badly on himself, his family, Islam and the Ismaili community. Aly had a liking for actresses. He dated Yvonne de Carlo below and then, after his acrimonious divorce from Rita, he often found himself caught by photographers in the company of Gene Tierney below left*

Popperfoto

before I saw, I am afraid, that they are not a well-assorted couple.'

In January 1953, Rita was awarded an uncontested Nevada divorce from the playboy Prince. The hearing took just 17 tense minutes, during which Rita was visibly on edge. She was granted custody of Yasmin, although she was still extremely afraid that Aly and his father might try to snatch her at any time. She was 34, and this was her third divorce.

On the rebound

Both Aly and Rita wasted no time in becoming romantically involved with other people. Aly began a highly publicized affair with another Hollywood actress, Gene Tierney. Once again, the Aga was horrified by his son's indiscretions. He reacted powerfully: 'If he marries Gene Tierney,' the old man angrily told Elsa Maxwell, 'my door will be closed to them both. He must respect his responsibilities to the Ismaili people. I have told him repeatedly I will not permit him to destroy our family heritage with indiscriminate marriages.' And there was more trouble in store, for although Rita and Aly were divorced they had still not reached a satisfactory agreement about Yasmin's future.

A disastrous choice

On 24 September 1953, on the anniversary of the day she had arrived in France to patch up her third marriage, Rita married an Argentine singer, Dick Haymes. Haymes was a disastrous choice. He drank heavily, had had two failed marriages himself, and was in deep trouble financially. His Hollywood nickname said it all: 'Mr Evil'. Within weeks of their wedding, Haymes slapped Rita in public as they were

AP/Wide World Photos

👑 *Rita successfully reclaimed custody of Rebecca* above *and Yasmin after they had briefly been made wards of court following allegations of lack of proper parental care*

seen quarrelling violently.

Yet somehow he managed to charm her. Rita was under considerable pressure at this time, for there had been three anonymous threats on Yasmin's life. These advised her to return to Aly, and bring up Yasmin in the Muslim faith — or else face the consequences. Haymes, meanwhile, was battling with immigration laws, the tax authorities and two ex-wives. It was not a pretty picture. Concerned about his daughter, Aly suggested that Rita send Yasmin to Paris where she would be safe. Rita, increasingly unstable, refused point blank. As Orson Welles was later to observe, 'After Aly, Rita was on a downward path, a steep, steep toboggan slide.'

Legal negotiations between Rita and Aly continued, complicated by an unpleasant case brought by the Society for the Prevention of Cruelty to Children. Rita was accused of neglecting her children by leaving them in the care of a friend while she went on holiday with Dick Haymes.

The Society had been alerted by neighbours, who felt that the girls were not being properly supervised. In addition, Rebecca had not been registered at any school. The girls were placed in protective custody after

---

TRAVELLING IN STYLE

© Martin Breese/Retrograph Archive Collection

The 1950s were the last decade of the great transatlantic liners. Cocooned in luxury, pampered by well-trained and numerous staff and crew, the well-heeled could cruise across the Atlantic in total comfort. The best of food and wine, top-class bands and cabaret entertained them, while they in turn entertained the world's press with their enormous mounds of baggage, expensive clothes and frequently scandalous love affairs.

To the companies that ran these great ships, the customer was always right – and if a passenger wanted to stay in the privacy of her cabin for the entire voyage, then she was entitled to the same impeccable service. Rita Hayworth, who crossed the Atlantic many times in the course of her stormy relationship with Aly Khan, often chose to do just that

two caseworkers had been to the house to investigate. The house soon became a tourist attraction; Rita's friend, Mrs Chambers, and the two girls remained inside with all the blinds pulled down. Orson Welles, Rebecca's father, made a public statement: 'Rita is not herself to blame, since she had always been a most devoted mother to both girls.'

Aly also loyally stood by her through this ordeal, but continued to press for Yasmin to be brought up as a Muslim, and to spend some time with him in Europe. He and Rita eventually reached an agreement in 1955, and Aly finally had a chance to get to know his daughter.

Her father's daughter

Five-year-old Yasmin delighted her father. Her dark brown eyes often sparkled with mischief, and she was always game for anything. Neglected or not, she was sensible and intelligent, and blessed with a sunny disposition.

Aly was even more captivated when he discovered that she shared his passion for horses. He taught her to ride a pony in Deauville, where he himself had learned all those years ago. Father and daughter rode along the white sands together, and he took the little girl to the races where she proudly applauded her father's horsemanship.

Although Yasmin continued to live with her mother and be educated in Beverly Hills, she visited her father almost every summer. He telephoned her frequently, showered her with presents, and kept a painting of her in his bedroom at the château. Despite that, Aly remained an absent father, for he could not spend much time with Yasmin – just as his father had

failed to spend much time with him. 'Aly was like Santa Claus,' said Rita. 'Whenever Yassy saw him, she'd see him for a day or two and he'd bring her a lot of presents, and then leave. He really loved her, but . . .'

Aly's new love

By the summer of 1955, Aly was involved with the woman who would be with him when he died. Her professional name was Bettina, although she had been born Simone Bodin 30 years earlier. This affair was yet another twist in the Prince's extraordinary destiny. Bettina – tall, slender and red-headed – had actually modelled Rita's wedding dress at the Fath salon.

♛ *Celebrations to mark the Aga Khan's 70 years as Imam were held in Bombay in 1957. Unfortunately, the Aga was too ill to attend and so it was necessary for Aly to deputize for him* above

'*As far as I am concerned we have no intention of breaking up*'

ALY

♛ *The Aga Khan III died in Switzerland in 1957 and his body was flown to Aswan, Egypt, to be housed temporarily in the grounds of his villa. Eighteen months later he was finally interred in the newly completed Aswan mausoleum, when a huge crowd gathered to witness the event* left

Robert Hunt Library

♔ Born on 28 December 1949, baby Yasmin already shows signs of inheriting her mother's beautiful eyes at just a few months old *left*

♔ *Below* At 18 months old Yasmin, a lively toddler, was happily unaware of the expensive and sensational divorce settlement between Aly and Rita that centred on her

Family Album

Aly and Rita's daughter, Princess Yasmin

UPI/Bettmann Newsphotos

♛ In 1957 Yasmin sailed again for Europe on board the *Ile de France* to spend her holidays with Aly Khan *left*. Like her parents, she was soon at home on luxury liners crossing the oceans

♛ By the age of nine Yasmin was an accomplished horsewoman. At her father's house in Deauville for the summer, she was able to ride on the beach for two hours each day *below*

♛ In Nice aged five, vivacious Yasmin gives a cheery grin for the camera *left*, the clockwork horse and jockey a reminder of her father's – and her own – interest in horses

👑 *Aly, the heir apparent, was passed over in favour of his son, Karim, who was named in the Aga's will as his successor. Although slighted, Aly supported Karim's nomination. In Syria, the Ismailis would have preferred Aly to be the new Aga, and when the Prince visited them to urge them to accept Karim, he was mobbed* above *by enthusiastic well-wishers*

'*After Aly, Rita was on a downward path, a steep, steep toboggan slide*'

ORSON

Aly could relax with Bettina, who was tender-hearted and undemanding. Unlike many of his other mistresses, Bettina never complained or asked for awkward explanations. The incorrigible Prince was, by now, set in his womanizing ways. 'I'm rather fond of this one, and I'm very, very fond of that one, and I must confess I rather love the one over there, so to keep them all happy, it is no great problem,' he said. Bettina's position resembled that of chief favourite in the harem.

It was Bettina who accompanied Aly when he entertained his daughter and step-daughter and who lived at Château de l'Horizon most of the time. During the last few years of his life, Aly managed to accommodate other women,
including the voluptuous platinum blonde actress Kim Novak and the mysterious, beautiful singer Juliette Greco.

Another divorce

On 4 November 1955, Rita filed for divorce from Dick Haymes on the grounds of 'extreme cruelty'. 'My husband used vile and abusive language to me ... I felt if I continued to live with him as his wife, my health would be permanently injured,' she claimed, and the divorce was granted the next month.

Rita was working hard once more, although the terrible strain of the past was beginning to show on her lovely face. The lighting had to be carefully manoeuvred, her make-up took hours to be just right, and the luminous love-goddess of old was struggling with her weight.

Her parts were changing, too. In *Pal Joey* (1957, also starring Frank Sinatra) Rita appeared as an older woman with a tangled past, involved in a love triangle with a younger girl, played – ironically – by Kim Novak. Later, in 1958, she gave one of the most poignant and painful performances of her career in *Separate Tables*. She played a sophisticated lonely woman who longed for love. '... Someone who was obviously seeking things that, after a number of unhappy, unfulfilled marriages, were not happening in her personal life ... I had a great sense that a lot of the truth of that performance came from Rita herself,' said her director, Delbert Mann.

Popperfoto

PAKISTAN'S AMBASSADOR

Controversy, Aly Khan's life-long companion, inevitably accompanied his official appointment as Pakistan's Ambassador to the United Nations in 1958. As some sections of the press pointed out, he was not even a citizen of the country, although he was soon seen in public sporting the uniform of a Pakistan army colonel. His turbulent sexual history and famous love of horse-racing were, once again, trotted out for the entertainment of more cautious mortals around the world.

But Aly surprised many of his detractors by taking his new responsibility very seriously, and working extremely hard. His natural talent as a party-giver was put to good use, while his urbane charm, polish and grace only highlighted his suitability as a diplomat. He moved into an apartment in New York, and installed both his talented Irish cook and his housekeeper.

By the time he came to make his first speech to the United Nations, he had studied Pakistan's problems thoroughly. His speech was well received, and by September he had been elected Vice-President of the General Assembly. Prince Aly Khan had proved his worth at last

Popperfoto

YEARS OF DECLINE

The late 1950s represented a very different turning-point in Aly's life. In the spring of 1957 he contacted Rita with an urgent message: the Aga Khan was seriously ill with pulmonary bronchitis, and longed to see his little grand-daughter again, for he believed that he was dying. Rita delayed Yasmin's trip until the summer when, she explained, she would have finished filming and could accompany her daughter. In the end, Yasmin travelled alone with her nanny that July.

Death of the Aga

After Yasmin had arrived in Switzerland, the Aga Khan III suffered a fatal heart attack. It was 11 July, and he was 79 years old. The Begum had sat at his bedside for 48 hours before his heart finally stopped beating. Weeping and shaken, Aly drove to the hotel where his daughter was staying. 'Grandpa has gone away from us,' he told her, and the little Princess sobbed in his arms.

A few days later came a second shock, when the Aga's will was formally read out. As the powerful old man's embalmed body lay in an upstairs room, the family's solicitor began: 'I Sultan Sir Mahomed Shah Aga Khan ... declare this to be my last will which I make this Twenty

Syndication International

♛ *Always one for the horses, Aly takes a ride with Bettina – his final constant companion – above at a garden party thrown by Mike Todd in Battersea in 1957 to advertise the London première of* **Around the World in Eighty Days**

♛ *Rita married film producer James Hill in February 1958. Although the couple looked happy enough when they visited London six weeks later* below, *happiness was to elude Rita once again*

fifth day of May One thousand nine hundred and fifty five ...' The man read on in an expectant silence; everyone was waiting for the crucial moment. At last it came: '... although he is not one of my heirs I appoint my grandson Karim the son of my son Aly Salomone Khan to succeed to the title of Aga Khan and to be the Imam and Pir of all my Shia Ismailian followers ...' The Aga had succeeded in having the final word – he had won his life-long battle with his impetuous son.

Aly never spoke of his feelings or disappointment. He hid behind a public smile, but his eyes were sad. Loyally he toured Ismaili centres in the East to introduce Karim, the new Aga. Two weeks after Karim, aged 21, had been enthroned in Karachi, Aly became Pakistan's Ambassador to the United Nations.

The beginning of the end

Rita, meanwhile, had married her fifth and final husband in February 1958. James Hill was a film producer who was reasonably successful, but very fond of drinking. He and Rita often over-indulged; there were spectacular rows, and any happiness was short-lived. Rita had become increasingly unpredictable, losing her temper over the smallest thing and growing forgetful and vague. Her destructive behaviour was naturally blamed on her drinking; while this certainly contributed, it was not the only reason for her tantrums. She had begun the painfully slow descent into premature senility. She had Alzheimer's disease.

In April 1960, Aly visited Yasmin in Los Angeles. Rita had become hostile towards him of late, but her new husband had persuaded her not to come between father and daughter. Aly was still travelling widely, but by May he was again back in Paris. On the evening of 12 May, the Prince climbed into his brand new Lancia with Bettina and a friend. They were on their way to have dinner, and Aly was driving as

Popperfoto

AP/Wide World Photos

👑 *Prince Aly Khan's restless life came abruptly to an end at the wheel of a new Lancia sports car when it crashed in May 1960 left. Rita Hayworth bottom outlived her third husband by 27 years, but she failed to find any measure of genuine* contentment. *Though her devoted daughter, Yasmin (below at her first marriage in 1985 to Basil Embiricos), tended her lovingly, the former 'Love Goddess' led an increasingly desperate existence – a victim of Alzheimer's disease*

Rex/Sipa

recklessly as ever: the Lancia collided head-on with an oncoming car. His passengers, and the other driver, were only slightly injured. Prince Aly Salomone Khan died in hospital just before midnight.

A devoted daughter

Rita Hayworth was to live on for another 27 years, working hard and making public appearances for many of them. But she grew increasingly unstable, and began to have serious difficulty with her lines as her memory degenerated. It was not until 1981 that her strange behaviour was publicly announced as resulting from Alzheimer's, a degenerative brain disease.

Princess Yasmin became her mother's official guardian. Mother and daughter lived in adjoining apartments off Central Park in New York. Yasmin cared for her mother tirelessly. 'She always had somebody come in to set her hair, do her makeup, and dress her,' said a close friend. The Princess also became a spokeswoman for the Alzheimer's Disease and Related Disorders Association. She organized annual fund-raising galas for them in her mother's honour, and worked hard to get publicity for this mysterious, incurable disease.

Yasmin found time to get married, in 1985, to a Greek shipping magnate, Basil Embiricos. Her son, Andrew, was born the following December but the marriage proved to be as brief as those her mother had entered into. (She has since married real-estate developer Christopher Jeffries.) The Princess and her baby remained in the apartment next door to Rita. Sadly, Rita was never aware of her new grandson, for by now she inhabited a twilight world of her own. On 14 May 1987, 27 years and two days after Aly's death, Rita Hayworth died, aged 68. She had found peace at last.

Rex Features

'*All I wanted was ... to be loved*'

RITA